A FIGHT
for
Religious Freedom

A FIGHT
for
Religious Freedom

A Lawyer's Personal Account of Copyrights,
Karma and Dharmic Litigation

JON R. PARSONS

Crystal Clarity Publishers
Nevada City, California

*Cover and interior design and layout by
Tejindra Scott Tully*

Parsons, Jon R., J. D.
    A Fight for Religious Freedom : a lawyer's personal account of copyrights, karma and dharmic litigation / Jon R. Parsons.
        p. cm.
    ISBN 978-1-56589-266-8 (pbk. : alk. paper) -- ISBN 978-1-56589-510-2 (epub)
1. Ananda Cooperative Village--Trials, litigation, etc. 2. Self-Realization Fellowship--Trials, litigation, etc. 3. Copyright--United States. 4. Freedom of religion--United States. 5. Religious communities--United States. 6. Yogananda, Paramahansa, 1893–1952. 7. Kriyananda, Swami. 8. Dharma. I. Title.

    KF225.A53P37 2012
    342.7308'52--dc23
            2012003499

www.crystalclarity.com
800-424-1055
clarity@crystalclarity.com

CONTENTS

Acknowledgments

Many people have helped to make this task a joyful journey. Liz, my wife through all of this and still there, has provided support in every way imaginable. Many have read and commented on the book, and made source materials available, including Jyotish and Devi Novak, Latika Parojinog, and Anandi Cornell. Elaine Geller provided invaluable comments and assistance during the book's formative stages; and I thank Mike and Cathie Foster (Carmel Valley) and Gary Grant / Maryann Shea (Nevada City) for letting me decamp to their homes and write, away from the work-a-day world. Richard Salva gave tirelessly of his time and talents to shepherd the work into final form, and Skip Barrett brought it to print with his gentle energy. But it could not have happened without the many members and supporters of the worldwide Ananda community, who impress and inspire me still; and their spiritual guide, Swami Kriyananda, who like his guru, surpasses description. I am blessed to live in a world that has such people in it.

PREFACE

The Fourth of July is a day when millions of Americans enjoy picnics, fireworks, and the general excitement over the birth of our nation. But in 2009, this national holiday was also celebrated on a much smaller scale for a different reason. Ananda World Brotherhood Village, an intentional community in Northern California, was founded on July 4, 1969, and was celebrating its fortieth anniversary on that day.

The event was reported in a local newspaper, *The Grass Valley Union:* "Forty years ago, a small band of people looking for meaning in their lives settled in a community on the San Juan Ridge where they could meditate, practice yoga and embark on a spiritual journey. The now-sprawling Ananda Village was the first of seven Ananda communities around the world founded on the principles of world peace among all people."

Sounds idyllic. But Ananda's forty-year history has been filled with challenges from the beginning—in fact, it has repeatedly been a struggle for survival, sometimes against overwhelming odds. Ananda was founded by Swami Kriyananda to carry out his guru, Paramhansa Yogananda's, mission to establish "World Brotherhood Colonies." In the first years the obstacles we faced, though challenging, were straightforward: creating an infrastructure, buildings, and homes on hundreds of acres of undeveloped land; working as best we could with conservative local forces who were trying to block us; and earning the funds to keep things going.

Paramhansa Yogananda's statement, "There are no obstacles, only opportunities," stood us in good stead in the early years. The community grew, and after seven years, we felt pretty confident that a solid foundation had been built.

Then disaster struck. On June 28, 1976, a small fire was ignited by sparks from an old county vehicle. The flames were fanned by strong winds and quickly spread in the dry grass and underbrush until it raged out of control. The fire consumed thousands of acres in the Northern California foothills, including most of Ananda's forests and structures.

With intense efforts over the next year, Ananda emerged phoenix-like from the ashes. In the period that followed, we not only rebuilt the community, but expanded it—establishing four new colonies along the West Coast, and later international ones in Italy and India. Once again our members, who by this time had dedicated over twenty years of their lives to Ananda, were confident that we were well on our way to fulfilling Yogananda's dream of spiritual communities.

Then in 1990 disaster struck again—this time not as a forest fire, but as a legal conflagration which threatened Ananda's existence more profoundly than any natural calamity. Self-Realization Fellowship (SRF), the organization founded by Paramhansa Yogananda in 1925, launched a complex and far-reaching legal attack against Ananda that ultimately lasted twelve years. The heart of their lawsuit, as the presiding judge, Edward Garcia, later observed was "to put Ananda out of business."

This book is the story of that battle, which was fought in the courts, in the press, on the Internet, in flyers dropped from airplanes, and ultimately on the steps of the United States Supreme Court.

Why are we writing this story of what, at first glance, might seem like just another sectarian squabble? The idea for the book emerged in this way:

By July 2001 many of us at Ananda were veterans of eleven years of intense legal battles: some had spent years doing legal research, others had been repeatedly questioned by hostile lawyers, or testified before a judge and jury. One evening for relaxation, Swami Kriyananda and a small group decided to see the documentary film, *Liberty! The American Revolution*. As we watched, we were struck by the similarities between the struggles of the early Americans with England and our own legal battles with SRF. At the end of the movie, we discussed the many common threads, and began to talk about what a great book the story of our lawsuit would make.

The similarities are truly striking:

a) The American Colonies and England shared a common cultural history, coming from the same "root stock" so to speak. Ananda, too, shared roots with SRF. Both groups followed the same guru, devoted themselves to the same spiritual practices, and were dedicated to sharing Yogananda's teachings with the world. Ananda's founder, Swami Kriyananda, had in fact once been on SRF's board of directors and had served as its vice-president.

But that was years in the past, and now stormy seas separated the two groups. In 1990 SRF declared it had exclusive rights to the "territory" of Paramhansa Yogananda—his name, his image, his words, and his teachings. And, like England, they were ready to wage war to maintain their control.

Ananda recognized behind the mask of SRF's legal proceedings and papers, the face of suppression and control. And, like the early Americans, the people of Ananda were ready to defend the principle of freedom, even to the point of putting their property and the life of Ananda at risk.

b) In the early days of the American Revolution, the war had gone poorly for the colonists as they faced the amassed power and wealth of England. Boasting the strongest army in the world, England quickly overwhelmed the colonists' untested military leaders and its ragamuffin band of volunteers.

SRF, too, had very deep pockets and employed the third largest law firm in America. A blitz of legal motions soon overwhelmed Ananda's lawyer (a sole practitioner without even a full-time secretary) and the inexperienced group of Ananda volunteers helping him.

We lost our first battle in court. The judge's initial ruling went against us—an important one that we feared would set the tone for the whole case. Overcoming a sense of being crushed before we had even begun, we managed to hang on, claw our way forward, and eventually to fight back. Ultimately, like General Washington, we achieved a near-miraculous victory.

c) At stake in the American Revolution was not just the outcome of a territorial dispute, but the issue of whether a new form of government—democracy, which was "of the people, by the people, and for the people"—could be created.

Kings and their cronies had decided the fate of nations for centuries. Similarly, SRF, as a monastic order, was under the absolute control of their president, Daya Mata, and her handpicked board of directors. No one else had "the right even to think," to quote a member of the board.

Ananda represented a new kind of spiritual organization. It, too, was a monastic order, but one in which all members' points of view were heard and respected. In a whimsical wordplay, Ananda termed its form of government a "dharmocracy," where decisions were based on *dharma*, or righteous action.

d) By far, the most important similarity was the shared fight for religious freedom. This legal and moral issue should have been resolved by the brilliant Constitution created by our Founding Fathers. But old ways of thinking die slowly, and religious freedom cannot simply be *declared*, any more than equality for women, freedom from slavery, or the right of all citizens to vote can be decreed by politicians.

New freedoms have to be won through determination and sacrifice. In our case, the fundamental question at the center of the legal battle was one of control: "Does an established church have the right to dictate how followers of a new expression of its teachings may or may not worship?"

Because we realized that this battle had broader implications than just our own lawsuit, we fought hard to defend and protect religious freedom and individual human rights. As our lead lawyer and the author of this book, Jon Parsons, told us, "I fully realize that this may well be the most important case of my career."

Here then, is a David and Goliath tale: the dramatic story of how a small group of people fought and won a victory against a seemingly unbeatable opponent. Our victory was not for ourselves alone, but one that may well protect the religious rights of future generations of Americans. Even now as we read the story, and relive in our minds the incidents that took place during that twelve-year ordeal, we are moved by feelings of deep gratitude that we were part of such a noble struggle—one proving that might does *not* make right, and that honor and integrity can, in the end, prevail.

Jyotish and Devi Novak
Ananda Village
Oct. 2, 2010

FOREWORD

"Oh, to have been a fly on the wall . . ." I had that pleasure once. During the years of hammer-and-tongs litigation between the Self-Realization Fellowship ("SRF") and the Ananda Church of Self-Realization lasting from 1990 to 2002, I was the principal outside legal counsel for Ananda and Swami Kriyananda. From that vantage point, I witnessed the events unfold, played some role in the developing drama, came to understand a bit about Yogananda, Kriyananda, and their mission, and saw SRF in action. Because a story about the heroic struggle for religious freedom is usually worth the telling, let me share with you some of what I remember from those exciting days.

It was a battle for Ananda's very survival. After years of effort and anxious uncertainty, and at great cost, we turned back SRF's attempt to "put Ananda out of business," as Judge Garcia once succinctly described it. That "business" was Ananda's mission to spread the writings and teachings of Paramhansa Yogananda (1893–1952), and to found "World Brotherhood Colonies" as Yogananda had urged. We did much more than defeat SRF's plans. In the process of preparing a defense we revealed SRF's feet of legal clay, and obtained court rulings and appellate opinions that placed numerous publications and photographs in the public domain. We stripped away SRF's registered trademarks of "Paramahansa Yogananda" and "Self-Realization," and reclaimed the ability of all followers to use Yogananda's name, voice, signature, photograph, and likeness in expressing his teachings.

The litigation morphed over the years into four lawsuits and two appeals, together with writ petitions to both the California Court of Appeal and the U.S. Supreme Court. Its web embraced the two churches and

Swami Kriyananda, as well as a former Ananda member, and the minister who spurned her. Ultimately, everyone who touched the case got named as a defendant in one lawsuit or another, and SRF found itself a defendant in its own sexual harassment suit. Our cosmic drama also spawned at least three other satellite lawsuits and two appeals involving star-crossed strangers, who inadvertently ventured too close to the litigation.

When the dust settled, Ananda was a spiritually richer community internationally recognized as a legitimate successor to Yogananda's legacy. Kriyananda had deepened a lifetime commitment to his Master, and re-invented ways of expressing that discipleship. Along the way, we freed up a large body of Yogananda's original writings and teachings for the world's edification and enjoyment. Ananda had weathered another crisis and come out stronger, and through that struggle laid the foundation for the florescence that followed. In these pages we revisit those days of struggle, doubt, commitment, and victory. I tell the tale, but the story is not mine. This story belongs to Kriyananda, the Ananda community he founded, and its many residents and members.

Chapter 1

CALLS AND LETTERS

1989–1990

These events started long before I ever heard of Ananda. Perhaps it began back in 1948 when Kriyananda first met Yogananda. Perhaps in 1955, when Daya Mata took over SRF's reins as its third president, or maybe in 1962, when she booted Kriyananda from the organization. Perhaps, as the parties all seemed to believe, it began lifetimes ago.

My involvement came much later, and by chance. By 1989 my law practice had grown to include a substantial amount of fair housing advocacy. That same year the Ananda Church leased a 72-unit apartment complex in neighboring Mountain View, then filled with tenants having no connection with the church. The church wanted to convert the entire complex into a religious community where Ananda members could live in harmony, chant, pray, meditate in small groups, and share vegetarian meals. The church hoped to make this transition happen with as little disruption to the current tenants as possible.

Sheila Rush, now known as Naidhruva, was then the Executive Director for the East Palo Alto Community Law Project, a non-profit legal clinic begun by students and faculty of nearby Stanford University. I helped out when I could with landlord-tenant matters, meeting with Law Project lawyers and clients at the old three-story home that the Project had converted into ramshackle offices. Sheila, a Harvard Law School graduate, ran an efficient operation on limited funds, and over the years we developed a cordial working relationship.

A Call from Sheila / Fall 1989

Until Sheila called me in 1989 to discuss representing the church, I didn't know she was an Ananda member. In fact, I had never heard of Ananda. While not religiously inclined, I have always considered myself "spiritual" in that fuzzy way people use the term to avoid the issue. As fate would have it my college years were spent studying Asian religions and philosophy. I had already read the Bhagavad Gita in different translations, some of the Upanishads, and even portions of the Vedas. The pantheon of Hindu deities were not strangers to me, and I had even dabbled in a little Ramakrishna, learning something about the Vedanta movement in America. Just enough knowledge to be dangerous.

During that first call Sheila started filling me in on what I needed to know about Ananda. It was a religious organization and a spiritual community founded in the 1960s by a Swami Kriyananda, also known as J. Donald Walters. Ananda was based, and most of its members resided, in an "intentional community" called Ananda Village, located in the Sierra Nevada Mountains of California, several miles north of Nevada City. In the 1980s Ananda began founding similar communities throughout the West, including the one now being formed in Mountain View. The residential community experience reflected Yogananda's belief that you should surround yourself with like-minded people seeking to know God through "simple living and high thinking." The residents and members tried to live lives that reflected, each day, the blend of Christian and Hindu-Yoga principles that Yogananda had brought to America in 1920. These practices included meditation, a vegetarian lifestyle, chanting, praying, and the complete avoidance of alcohol and recreational drugs. Sheila explained that the residential community in Mountain View was another little step in making the world a better place.

It sounded good to me. A church was legally permitted to establish housing for its members' use and benefit, and then rent to those members without violating fair housing laws. As a community of sincere believers, Ananda could exercise those religious freedoms permitted under both federal and state law. We thought that if we were legally careful and politically savvy, we could convert the apartment complex into a religious community without it blowing up in our face.

A church taking over a large apartment complex can trigger local opposition, and more so when the church is not one of the mainstream denominations. We talked about possible political pressure from the current residents, flak in the press, and the bias against newer religions in a religious America. It was important to Ananda that the transition be done in a "dharmic" manner. Sheila explained that by "dharmic" she meant actions that were morally correct, ethically proper. We were dealing with people's lives, and in achieving our goal of a better world, we should do as little harm as possible to a tenant's current existence. It might take a little longer, or cost a little more, but we were to minimize disruption to the existing tenants. Correct action regardless of cost, proper conduct despite the consequences. You could not be blind to the cost and effect of what you did, but you kept your eye on doing the right thing.

We arranged that current tenants had all the time they wanted to move out. But when they did vacate, their units would then be rented to Ananda members. The church also immediately made improvements to the property that accentuated its religious character such as devotional statues, shrines, and a chapel. These improved the ambiance for resident members, and reminded the non-members that they were now living in a more refined and spiritual environment. As Ananda members moved in, the spirit of the community changed, and the natural dynamic from that like-minded energy sped up the transition without Ananda having to evict anyone.

The law is not always intuitive, however, and this "dharmic" solution actually exposed the church to some risk of litigation. The Fair Housing Act permits a church to discriminate in favor of its members only for housing which it "owns or operates for other than a commercial purpose." When the church allowed non-members to continue to reside in their units as long as they wanted, and pay rent, that kindness raised a question whether the complex was then being operated for a "commercial purpose." The safer route would have been for the church to immediately evict all non-members, and I appreciated that Ananda was willing to stand by its beliefs in the face of this risk. Despite the old saw, it seems that some good deeds do go unpunished, and the transition proceeded smoothly. Everyone ended up as happy as could be hoped for, with a harmonious resolution to a problematic situation. I closed my file, and figured that was the last I would hear from these good people.

Sheila Calls Again / February 1990

A few months later Sheila called again. Kriyananda had received a threatening letter from SRF's lawyers in Los Angeles, and wondered if he could discuss it with me. Of course, I would be pleased to talk with him about it, without the slightest idea yet of what might be involved. "It" turned out to be the first step of an amazing adventure that would change many lives, including my own. But at first it was just about a name.

Sheila again provided background. In December 1968 Kriyananda incorporated the entity we now know as Ananda under the name The Yoga Fellowship. By the mid-1980s, the name had been changed to the Fellowship of Inner Communion. Recently, Kriyananda and the community had been searching for a name that better described what he saw to be Ananda's current mission, a mission developing over time. Following a community meeting in early January 1990, the membership voted to change the church's name to the Church of Self-Realization.

SRF, perched atop Mt. Washington in Los Angeles, was not pleased. Yogananda had founded SRF in 1935, and the organization assumed Yogananda's mantle when he passed away in 1952. SRF thought Ananda's new name sounded too similar to its own, and told its lawyers to make Ananda stop using "Self-Realization" as part of its name. Their letter had triggered Sheila's call.

Sheila gave me the back-story to Ananda's name change and SRF's reaction. It seems that Kriyananda had joined SRF in 1948 and become particularly close to Yogananda during the last four years of his life. They spent time together at Yogananda's desert retreat at Twentynine Palms, where they and Laurie Pratt, later called Tara Mata, worked on Yoga-

18

nanda's final editing of several key works. For ten years after Yogananda's passing in 1952, Kriyananda continued serving Yogananda within the SRF organization. He rose to the position of vice-president, was a member of the board of directors, and headed up the monks on a day-to-day basis. He spoke several languages, and by the early sixties was serving overseas as SRF's principal representative in India. In 1962 he was unexpectedly summoned to New York City. After he checked into the designated hotel and retired for the night, someone slipped a note under his door. That note informed him that he was fired from the board, expelled from SRF, and instructed to leave. Just like that. Without warning or explanation. After 14 years as a monk. He had grown penniless in SRF's service, and he didn't even get a face-to-face "Sorry, but it's not working out." No "Thank you for years of loyal and unpaid service." During a devastating session the next day with SRF's president, Daya Mata, and Tara Mata, Kriyananda learned that he must sever all connection with SRF, and could have nothing further to do with Yogananda. He could not use Yogananda's teachings or SRF's materials, and was forbidden from holding himself out as one of Yogananda's disciples. They slipped him a check for $500.00 and showed him the door. Over the years, whenever SRF leadership would be asked about Kriyananda's ouster, the stock response was "If you only knew!" It was always rhetorical. If anyone really knew anything they were not telling. During the litigation it became clear that the ladies who then ran the organization had issues with Kriyananda's charismatic and eloquent leadership. Photos from those days show a fit and handsome Kriyananda sporting a neatly trimmed beard, looking quite the man's man in what must have been a henhouse. Their differences on the board had found expression in ways that went to the essence of Yogananda's mission. The women wanted to protect the legacy of their days with Yogananda by sanitizing and preserving his memory, while Kriyananda advocated a more dynamic application of Yogananda's teachings to a changing world. Kriyananda would not be dissuaded, so he had to go.

After mourning and reflecting on this unexpected turn, and with no other avenue to express his devotion, Kriyananda decided to begin teaching yoga and meditation in the San Francisco Bay Area. It was the mid-1960s and the San Francisco area provided fertile grounds for New Age religions. Through lectures and classes Kriyananda attracted both students and funding, and before long he had obtained some acreage up country in Nevada County. There he would found the community we now know as Ananda Village. The first World Brotherhood Colony embodying Yogananda's teachings.

Through the 1980s Kriyananda tried to avoid upsetting SRF, and steered Ananda in directions that would not conflict with what SRF was doing. When he founded his own organization in the 1960s he named it The Yoga Fellowship, later changing the name to the Fellowship of Inner Communion, to avoid any similarity with SRF's or Yogananda's names. In his futile attempts to establish a harmonious relationship with SRF, Kriyananda offered to give the entire Ananda Village to SRF. Three times. The SRF Board would have nothing to do with any community that Kriyananda had founded.

Over the years Kriyananda and the Ananda community came to realize that regardless what they did, or did not do, there would be no rapprochement with SRF. At a lengthy and lively meeting in January 1990, the community decided it was time to act. That action included adding "Self-Realization" to the church's name, as an expression of Ananda's ultimate spiritual goal. Yogananda had called his religion "Self-realization." Ananda had matured as a vehicle of Yogananda's teaching, and it appeared proper that Ananda now embrace a name that truly expressed its religious path. Within days the Fellowship of Inner Communion had become The Church of Self-Realization. SRF heard immediately about Ananda's declaration of spiritual independence, and now, weeks later, SRF was threatening to file suit.

Sheila told me more about Kriyananda, who she called "Swami." He authored numerous books and songs, lectured in several languages, and provided the channel through which the community received the teachings and blessing of Yogananda, who was their guru. In Kriyananda, she explained, beat the strong heart of Ananda, and most Ananda members looked to him as spiritual guide and a living inspiration. During our conversation she repeated that Yogananda, not Kriyananda, was the "guru," but it would be a while before I fully understood the significance of her comment. There were questions about the legal direction the mission should take, and Ananda needed to see if its legal standing was as strong as its moral commitment. I would be happy to review the letter and share my thoughts. Sheila would send over a copy and set up the call.

First impressions are important, and Gibson, Dunn and Crutcher's letterhead comprised august-sounding names crawling down a full quarter of the first page, engraved in a dark serif font. The February 9, 1990 letter came right to the point. Ananda must change its name, back to what it was, or to something else, but nothing close to anything sounding like "Self-realization." The letter raised this single point—that the Ananda Church was not to use "Self-realization" as part of its name.

Nasty-grams from lawyers follow a standard formula: a situation is stated in language as favorable to the client's interests as possible, and then some action is demanded on the recipient's part, who is warned that failure to act will have dire consequences. The author vouches the inevitability of his client's victory, and often expresses personal disdain for the recipient's knowing and intentional misconduct. This February 9th letter was no different, and finished with a big bold signature, showing its author meant business and should be taken seriously. Although Gibson, Dunn and Crutcher was one of the largest law firms in the world, employing legions, I thought I could handle a dispute over a church's name. I had already handled several trade name issues in state court and felt I could quickly get up to speed on the religious context. How complicated could it be? I made a few notes on points to discuss, and was eager to talk.

Swami Kriyananda / February 1990

One does not run into many swamis on the South Side of Chicago, where I grew up, and I was uncertain about the etiquette. I asked Sheila what I should call him, how to act, and whether there was any protocol to be followed when talking with a swami. She said not to worry about it. And, as it turned out, Kriyananda didn't care about those things either. Before the case ended there would be much made about the use and meaning of the term "Swami." But like many who respect the man, his wit and charm, without being Ananda members, I too quickly came to call him Swami.

Naturally, I had done some research on Kriyananda before our call. J. Donald Walters was born in Romania in 1926 of American parents, and educated at the best schools. Living in New York in 1948, he came across a copy of Yogananda's *Autobiography of a Yogi* that had been published two years earlier. Reading it through in one sitting, he got on a bus and rode cross-country to Los Angeles. Once there, Kriyananda immediately tracked Yogananda down at one of SRF's temples, was accepted as a disciple by Yogananda on the spot, and pledged his lifelong loyalty and support. Soon after, Kriyananda became a trusted assistant to Yogananda, who placed him in charge of the monks. These independent sources confirmed what Sheila had told me about Kriyananda's background, his editing Yogananda's works under Yogananda's personal guidance, and Kriyananda's role at SRF after 1952. The public record went silent about what happened in the early 1960s and picked up again only years later with articles about the Village. Having read what I could find, Kriyananda seemed the real deal, but I still didn't know what to make of it all. I expected anything from a commanding captain of industry to a shell-shocked foot soldier of God.

When we talked it became clear that Kriyananda was "none of the above." There was a gentleness and innocence in the way he spoke. An almost childlike simplicity in his explanations, shared in a slow and deliberate way that might have sounded pedantic were he not so warm and engaging. He told me more about his involvement with SRF and his separation. He talked about Yogananda's mission to America, SRF and its current leadership, and his vision of Ananda's role in Yogananda's legacy. After catching me up on the last forty years, he turned to the lawsuit. We discussed the uncertainty of litigation, the misfit between law and religion, and how lawsuits should be avoided if at all possible.

Kriyananda acknowledged the legal brambles, and that a judge might be put in charge of the future of both churches. It was important that I understood, however, that the real fight was not about a change of name. It was about the struggle for religious freedom, and specifically Ananda's freedom from SRF's religious control, if not tyranny. Although this karmic adventure would take place inside a courtroom, it was not really about the law. It was all about spiritual growth, like tendrils that clamber toward the light. There was talk of will, duty, and destiny. I thought that all well and good, and looked forward to an insight or two. But this was litigation in federal court, and serious business. We finished up talking about the brutal and costly reality of litigation. Even a relatively simple dispute about a name change could last for two, or even three, years in federal court and easily end up costing six figures. "Six figures" was my oblique way of saying it would cost a lot of money. I had no idea then that the lawsuit would acquire a life of its own, but SRF had hired "Gibson Dunn," and I knew it would not be cheap. Kriyananda ended the conversation by observing that sometimes you must pay for your principles, at which point I agreed to prepare a response to the letter, and be available as needed.

The Ranks Array / March–June 1990

We replied to SRF's letter a few days later, pointing out that within the Hindu-Yoga tradition the phrase "Self-realization" describes the ultimate goal of union with God, and is therefore generic when used in the name of a church. We explained our position that, like with "salvation" or "redemption" in the Christian context, any church may use a generic term that accurately describes its mission or its teachings. As a church whose spiritual goal was "Self-realization" resulting in union with God, Ananda had the right to use the term "Self-realization" in its name. Kriyananda and the church might have held off exercising their rights out of unrequited respect, but they had not given up those rights, and could exercise them now.

We attempted to show both the reasonableness of Ananda's position and the larger issues at stake. It was a matter of religious freedom and constitutional rights. Ananda even proposed a compromise, and offered to use the name "Ananda Church of Self-Realization." We thought our response fair and rather conciliatory, based on principles that SRF should also recognize.

SRF's lawyers replied later that month, rejecting out of hand that "Self-realization" was in any way generic, calling Kriyananda an "interloper," and reiterating their demand that Ananda never use any language in its church name that looked or sounded like "Self-realization." If Ananda did not concede this point and immediately change its name from Church of Self-Realization, then a lawsuit would surely follow. It was just a name, but apparently important to SRF.

Ananda also felt strongly on the issue. As legitimate disciples of Yogananda, the Ananda community should also be able to use the name that Yogananda had chosen to describe his vision of the ultimate goal of Yoga. Given the narrow scope of the issue, and now confident their use of "Self-realization" was legal, Ananda decided to stand on principle. Beginning with Ananda's founding in the late 1960s, SRF had always publicly ignored Ananda, while keeping close tabs on its activities, privately criticizing its plans, and interfering with those plans when it could. Kriyananda had repeatedly given in to SRF's wishes, but feckless deference did not seem to be working. The time had come to take a stand.

It was also far from clear that SRF would actually sue, as SRF had already backed down after making legal threats. Years earlier SRF had threatened a lawsuit against the Amrita Foundation in Texas for reprinting some early Yogananda texts. SRF backtracked when it discovered that many of those early interpretations of Biblical passages published by Amrita had already slipped into the public domain. Another dust-up had swirled around Ananda Publications' publishing of *Stories of Mukunda* in 1976. Ananda Publications (later, Crystal Clarity Publishers) was Ananda's publishing arm, and at that time Kriyananda wrote most of its releases.

Brother Kriyananda, as he was known at SRF, had written *Stories of Mukunda* while still a monk there. He printed it privately in December

1953, and distributed copies to his brother monks as Christmas presents that year. SRF published a copy of the work, and advertised it for a while in *Self-Realization Magazine*, but by the 1970s the work had long gone out of print. When Ananda Publications republished a copy of the book in 1976, SRF sent Kriyananda and Ananda Publications a "cease and desist" letter. Kriyananda responded that he would not stop publishing his own writings, and a second printing ensued in 1977. SRF did nothing.

With this past history, maybe SRF's most recent threat was just more talk. Maybe SRF would grumble and go away. It seemed likely. How upset could SRF really be about Ananda calling itself "Church of Self-Realization?" What was the harm? What were the damages?

In February and March 1990, while we were dealing with SRF's first letter to Kriyananda, SRF had begun secretly preparing for a much larger lawsuit. SRF quietly applied to the U.S. Patent and Trademark Office to register the terms "Self-Realization Fellowship," "Self-Realization Fellowship Church," and "Paramahansa Yogananda" as trademarks and service marks. Parallel applications were filed with the California Secretary of State in Sacramento. While still corresponding with Ananda about the church's name, SRF was already appropriating Yogananda's name and title as a registered brand name to use for the sale of SRF's goods and services. SRF also registered the term "Self-realization" as a unique form of religious expression that could only be used by SRF. The monks and nuns had begun assembling hundreds of pages of exhibits to show that Ananda quoted extensively from Yogananda's talks and writings. Each quote would result in a claim of copyright infringement. In those halcyon months from March to July 1990, Ananda basked in the dusty heat of the high Sierras, and the last calm days of the millennium, unaware of the game already afoot.

Chapter 2

THE HERALD OF WAR

July 1990

The bad news of a lawsuit must be delivered in person to each defendant in the form of a Summons and Complaint. The bearer is usually a professional process server, often paid at a flat rate. By the time SRF's server found his way to Ananda Village on Tyler Foote Road off Highway 49, down and up curvy mountain roads for twenty miles north from Nevada City, he had earned his fee. The northern Sierra Nevada Mountains grow hot and dry in the summer, the dust from gravel roads hanging in the air long after a car has passed. Once you make it to the Village, it is hard to know which road to take to what housing cluster or home to find a particular person. In 1990 most of the roads were not paved, and there were no maps or guideposts to assist the first-time visitor. But Ananda was served.

The complaint Sheila forwarded to me bore little resemblance to the letters that preceded it. No longer a dispute about a name, this lawsuit sought nothing less than to eliminate Ananda as a religious competitor. The complaint ran 48 pages, with another 163 pages of exhibits, and asserted 9 different "claims for relief." Only two of those claims concerned the church's name. And SRF had alleged copyright and trademark infringement, making a federal case out of it, and requiring the complaint be filed in the District Court for the Eastern District of California, located in Sacramento. The pleading presented a laundry list of alleged wrongdoing that was never mentioned in the letters, with some claims stated several different ways for maximum effect. SRF now claimed that:

1. Ananda "falsely described" its "goods and services" with a "false designation of origin," in violation of federal law;

2. Ananda had infringed SRF's "Self-Realization" trademark and its "Paramahansa Yogananda" service mark by using those terms, and Ananda's use had "diluted" or "tarnished" SRF's marks;

3. Ananda also infringed SRF's copyrights by quoting things that Yogananda had said in numerous books, magazines, and talks;

4. Ananda violated SRF's exclusive right to use the "name, voice, signature, photograph, and likeness" of Yogananda, who was a "deceased personality" as defined by statute;

5. Ananda copied and distributed, and thereby infringed, seven recordings of Yogananda's talks made between November 20, 1949 and January 5, 1952; and

6. Ananda used the name "Church of Self-Realization" as a form of "deceptive advertising, unfair business practices, and unfair competition."

SRF asked the court to order that all of Ananda's income from the sale of its books, tapes, and services be gathered together and held in trust for SRF's benefit. Whatever money Ananda might be making, SRF argued, was attributable to Ananda's breach of one or another of SRF's rights, and Ananda should not be spending this money, but preserving it to turn over to SRF later. To find out how much money that was, SRF needed to do an "independent accounting" of both Ananda's and Kriyananda's finances.

SRF requested the court award millions of dollars in damages, and more for punitive damages, against both Ananda and Kriyananda. In addition, at least two injunctions were needed; one right away, and then a permanent one later, prohibiting Kriyananda and Ananda from ever holding themselves out as teaching anything by or about Yogananda. SRF wanted Ananda and Kriyananda to be prohibited from ever using the term "Self-Realization" to describe their religious teachings, and in particular from using the term in Ananda's name.

Despite complaining about copyright infringements too numerous to list, the complaint made no allegation about any infringement of the *Autobiography of a Yogi*, Yogananda's principal work. Ananda had quoted from it on many occasions, and we were surprised and relieved to see that it was not included. At least we would not need to deal with the *Autobiography*.

In a paragraph emblematic of SRF's vision of itself, the complaint claimed that Yogananda had founded SRF, "under the control and direction of its President and Board of Directors, as the organ through which he desired and intended to promulgate the principles and teachings which he espoused." Thus, from the beginning of the suit SRF inflated the importance of the corporation, and minimized the role of Yogananda outside the organization. While it was true, as the complaint alleged, that Yogananda was president of SRF for life, he was so much more. He was the guru-preceptor and Self-realized master. He had formed SRF, as well as other organizations, to serve him, not vice-versa. SRF's myopic perception of its importance would color positions it took throughout the lawsuit.

One church suing another to stop it spreading the teachings of the guru they both followed did not seem dharmic, but what did I know? If SRF didn't want to establish World Brotherhood Colonies, why not let Ananda do it? And SRF's claims to control the purity of the teachings seemed like sweeping back the tide, as if any organization could now control religious doctrine for long. If there was any question about Yogananda's actual words and the "purity" of SRF's version of those teachings, all SRF had to do was trot out its archived originals. SRF had grown rich as Croesus over the years and could not have been hurt economically by Ananda's activities. Before Yogananda's passing, he had famously commented that once he was gone "only love" could take his place. SRF apparently believed in tough love. To make matters worse, we learned from the complaint that SRF had also retained Downey Brand, the largest law firm in Sacramento, to be their hometown boys.

The expanded scope of the lawsuit made us stop and reconsider everything. We reviewed each claim to see what we knew about the facts alleged, and what defenses might be available. It would be costly to guess wrong. But we were plunging too quickly into waters too deep to know our way out yet. If it was illegal for Kriyananda and Ananda to quote their guru, then they were indeed in trouble. But giving up would not solve that problem. Kriyananda could not believe that his guru meant him to be silent. Forward lay the way to the light and I was to blaze the legal path.

With the ranks thus arrayed, *gurubais* on both sides, the parties agreed to a final meeting to try and avoid the crisis. Even on the eve of a battle one might come to see things in new ways.

Fresno / August 1990

Fresno was a bustling farm town of a quarter million souls, nestled in the southern reaches of the verdant San Joaquin Valley. Known mainly as the home of the Sun-Maid Raisin processing plant, Fresno also provided the last city stop on the road to the Sierra Nevada Mountains and Yosemite National Park. And it happened to sit halfway between the northern Gold Country home of Ananda and the Los Angeles headquarters of SRF. The parties would meet at a downtown hotel, with all the principals present, for a candid discussion on the important issues underlying the complaint. It would start with prayer and chanting, and who knew where it might go?

Living in Palo Alto, I drove separately to Fresno the night before. I had nothing to say, and went only because I had to be there as Ananda's counsel to help finalize any agreement the parties might happily make. Six months before I didn't know a thing about SRF. Now, at this meeting, I was going to put faces to the names and personalities I had lately learned so much about. Daya Mata, the third and current president of the organization, her sister Ananda Mata, as well as other "direct disciples" like Uma Mata and Mrinalini Mata, would be there.

During a trip to India in the late 1950s, someone told Sister Daya, as she was then known, that "Sister" did not sound distinguished enough for the head of Yogananda's organization. After she returned to California, the board held a meeting and the female direct disciples awarded themselves each the honorary title of Mata (Sanskrit for "mother"), with colorful *saris* to match. Faye's sister Virginia, already long known as Mataji, received the new name of Ananda Mata. Some of the monks at SRF had been direct disciples too, including Kriyananda, but they must be content remaining "Brothers." SRF had become a matriarchy.

On the way to Fresno I passed Christopher Ranch, known worldwide for its garlic, and whose patriarch was one of the founders of the annual Gilroy Garlic Festival. Seven years later a family member, attorney Rob Christopher, would join the Ananda litigation team, and head up the 2002 trial in Sacramento. As the Central Valley unfolded verdant and green, a golden sun setting behind me, I was at peace with the world. And what a world, that I should find myself driving to such a meeting in Fresno. These ladies had each been meditating long hours every day for the last sixty years or so, and collectively carried the wisdom from centuries of studying the teachings. They must be buzzing with their Master's energy. I wondered if I'd feel it when they entered the room. This was going to be fun.

The meeting next morning was not fun. Daya Mata and Ananda Mata led the SRF delegation, and conferred from time to time with their sister Matas. Some monks were also in attendance, but with no apparent input into what was going on. We had prepared for the meeting with detailed settlement suggestions, written negotiating points, and "fall-back" positions. It was a last chance to avoid the cost and chaos of litigation, and we took it seriously. A large conference room had been reserved, with a table at one end, and after introductions we all took our seats. It started well enough, with Daya Mata leading a prayer and then some let's-get-comfortable group chanting. Ananda opened the working session of the meeting by offering to give ground and use "God-Realization" instead of "Self-Realization" in its name. A major concession. This was all the letters had asked.

But now the lawsuit embraced much more. SRF would not budge from its expanded demands stated in the complaint. It quickly became apparent that SRF looked upon Fresno as the last opportunity for an errant disciple to "come to Canossa" and kneel in the snow of their love and forgiveness. If Kriyananda stopped using "Self-Realization" and his Master's name, and disavowed any connection to his Master's line of teaching, then he could go in peace. The meeting was over as soon as it began, but dragged on for hours as Ananda probed in vain for some compromise. There had been no buzz, and it seemed a long drive with little to show for it. But I had seen the assembled Matas strut their stuff, playing oriental in their pastel *saris*. It had been all decorous and polite, and the ladies seemed nice enough, but when Fresno failed they let slip the dogs of law.

SRF Makes Its Move / September 1990

SRF filed a motion for a preliminary injunction in September 1990, the month before our first scheduled court appearance. It asked the court to enjoin, or prohibit, Ananda from using not only the name "Church of Self-Realization," but also the "service mark" Paramahansa Yogananda. Ananda should not be able to use Yogananda's name in connection with the sale of goods or services—by which SRF meant Ananda's religious services and programs. This was the first of many motions that explained SRF's mission in purely commercial terms. SRF could have been selling "Yogananda" brand shoes as well as Self-realization—it was all about the brand.

SRF's motion included a declaration from a Carolyn McKean of Portland, Oregon. Her declaration stated that she had once bought something from Ananda thinking she was buying it from SRF, and when she called Ananda to clarify, she became confused. This declaration provided the lynchpin for SRF's claim that Ananda was intentionally trying to pass itself off as being affiliated with SRF. SRF also offered this evidence to show that consumers were confused by the similarity in the names of the two organizations. Just before, and for a while after, the McKean declaration Ananda had been receiving telephone calls from people who would state that they were confused about the differences between SRF and Ananda, and ask if the two organizations were the same, or affiliated in some way. The calls were so suddenly numerous, and surprisingly similar, that we knew SRF had some new iron in the fire. Ananda members who staffed the telephones were advised to answer all inquiries truthfully, but carefully, and keep track of all calls concerning confusion. After about six months, when the callers failed to glean any misstatements that SRF could use to advantage, the calls stopped as suddenly as they had begun.

We responded to SRF's request for an injunction with what we had, but it amounted to simply denying SRF's evidence and pointing to the Constitution. Without yet obtaining any information from SRF, we could only react to what SRF said. The allegations were so numerous and the issues so unusual that I could not grasp them quickly or well enough. We submitted our papers and hoped for the best.

The First Courthouse / October 1990

The Federal Courthouse in Sacramento was in the middle of its own changes, and in 1990 consisted of temporary chambers on several floors in a converted office building on Capitol Mall, a few blocks down from the Capitol Building. The retrofit showed its age but would have to do until the new courthouse could be built. For much of the case, therefore, we stayed at the Holiday Inn on J Street in preparation for our early morning court appearances. We would meet in the hotel restaurant before each session for breakfast and some last minute strategizing. I enjoyed the five-block walk en masse to court, the Capitol gleaming under the morning sun. Good times. Our case lasted so long that when the trial took place twelve years later, it would be on the eighth floor of the new Federal Courthouse.

In the Federal District Court a new case filing is randomly assigned to a judge, who thereafter handles all aspects of the case from hearings and rulings along the way, to the trial itself. If a case is sent back to the trial court after appeal, it returns to the same judge. Federal judges are appointed by the president, and once approved by Congress they serve for life. Given their tenure and power, they often develop into independent thinkers with forceful personalities.

On the morning of October 12, 1990, we stood for the first time before Judge Edward J. Garcia, and took the measure of the man who would decide Ananda's fate. Garcia had then been a federal judge for six years. He started off in the Sacramento County D.A.'s office, and rose to become Chief Deputy District Attorney. Governor Reagan appointed him to the Municipal Court in 1972, and twelve years later President Reagan elevated him to the federal bench for life. Raised in the Sacramento area, Garcia played baseball as a kid on the north side of town. Even in his sixties he swung a mean bat. The available published profile of Garcia painted a picture of an old school, no-nonsense judge who controlled his courtroom with a stern demeanor. He was known to have reduced counsel to tears, and to hold strong opinions of cases and lawyers who appeared before him. We were concerned that if he formed an initial negative opinion of Ananda we would have a hard time turning him around.

True to reports, Garcia ruled his demesne with sharp eyes and cutting words. His massive wooden bench seemed taller, more formidable, than usual. And he did not suffer fools, or coddle the inexperienced, or anyone else who showed less that complete candor. Our matter came up later on that morning's calendar, so we had an opportunity that first day to see him dressing down lawyers to the point that one indeed started to cry. Yikes. I never breathed easy in front of Garcia, even later in the case when he was consistently ruling in our favor. But I appreciated the speed and efficiency with which he handled a heavy caseload. He would complain from the bench about the length of our papers, and threaten to impose page limits on the next filing, but he never did. He read everything we gave him and gave us back detailed and considered opinions.

Chapter 3
STUMBLING OFF THE BLOCK
October 1990

We had not anticipated such an omnibus complaint, and before we could come to grips with it, SRF followed up with a well-crafted motion for a preliminary injunction. This motion clearly had been in the works for some time, and painted the parties as simple business competitors, in the niche market of Yogananda-branded Self-realization goods and services. SRF claimed to own all the tangible and intangible rights concerning Yogananda, and portrayed Ananda and Kriyananda as late-on-the-scene infringers. Ananda was supposedly pretending to be affiliated with SRF, while Kriyananda was selling some second-rate religious product pretending to be SRF's real McCoy. SRF said it needed an injunction to stop Ananda's palming off, and to staunch the damages that would otherwise flow from acts of infringement "too numerous to recite." The motion may have been smoke and mirrors but our response failed to persuade.

Garcia Gives SRF an Injunction / October 1990

That October morning Garcia granted most of SRF's requested injunction. He ordered that, until time of trial, Ananda could not (1) use "for any purpose whatsoever" the name "Church of Self-Realization" or any other name similar to SRF's various Self-Realization and Yogoda Sat-Sanga names, or (2) use the name Paramahansa or Paramhansa Yogananda "as or in connection with the name of defendant's organization."

Ananda must change its name and be very careful about its new one.

On a happier note, Garcia did *not* grant SRF's request for an injunction preventing Ananda from using any of the works in which SRF claimed to hold a copyright. Garcia later explained that he felt "compelled" to limit the injunction in this way because that portion of the relief could "curtail defendants' religious practices." This proviso was important, but little comfort in the moment.

We conducted a post-mortem of the ruling over lunch and I gave the necessary analysis of this major setback early in the case. Judges do not hand out injunctions for the asking, and Garcia's ruling indicated he thought SRF had a good case. He had already determined that SRF would probably win, and that it needed immediate protection against Ananda. We were in trouble. To win now, we must convince Garcia that his initial take on the situation was wrong. Although SRF, as the plaintiff, still carried the burden of proof for each of its claims, that burden had now effectively shifted to Ananda. Before departing our separate ways that day we agreed to think through the next steps carefully, and talk soon.

My route back to the office through Stockton gave me a good two hours for tortured introspection. I had been entrusted with an almost sacred task, and stumbled badly. If these Ananda people thought I could help them, maybe they were not as smart as they looked. They had backed the wrong horse, but luckily we were not yet midstream. How could I have been so wrong, and SRF now so close to victory?

Garcia's follow-up written order in November provided the opportunity for a heart-to-heart talk with Kriyananda and the community leaders about how the case was too much for me. We found ourselves pitted against two giant firms while I was struggling to understand decades of history and complicated federal and state legal issues about nine different claims. It was too daunting, and more than I, a sole practitioner, should even attempt to handle. In fact, to put it bluntly, I had been "outgunned." There is no dishonor in acknowledging reality, and regrettably, I must step aside, but would be happy to help in the search for a more suitable firm.

Kriyananda responded that they understood the personnel imbalance, and how we needed more warm bodies on Ananda's side of the legal table. But Kriyananda saw something happening that I did not, and he wanted me to stay. It wasn't about me, he explained. It was about what God and guru were doing here, and I guess I was a cog in that bigger machine. Still, they should have replaced me. But Kriyananda wanted me to stay because, in his words, I was "dharmic" and a "man of integrity," and I could hardly disagree.

Instead, I would be given help. Ananda put together a "legal team" consisting of Kriyananda, Jyotish and Devi Novak, Vidura and Durga Smallen, and David and Asha Praver. This team played an active role throughout the case: discussing and deciding strategy, assembling financial and other resources, and actively communicating with the wider Ananda world. Sheila would be made available to assist on what quickly became a full-time basis. And, we had a new support team. Cathy Parojinog (who is now known as Latika) and Keshava Taylor would provide research, organization, and support services, often heading up a bevy of volunteers who handled the copying, collation, and delivery of documents. Brothers and sisters in arms.

SRF Tries to Gild the Lily / August 1991

SRF liked the way Garcia seemed to be leaning, and tried to push him a little farther. In August 1991, they surprised us with a motion to expand the scope of the preliminary injunction. In response to the injunction Ananda had changed its announcements, and now advertised its church services using the name "Church of God-Realization," with Yogananda's name and picture appearing somewhere on the ad. Ananda was careful, however, that Yogananda's name was not used "in connection with the name of defendant's organization." SRF did not like Ananda's continued use of the Master's name in any form, and collected a number of Ananda advertisements from the various colonies. SRF claimed that these showed Ananda's use of "Yogananda's name in close proximity with defendants' name." While this conduct did not violate the language of the injunction, SRF claimed these ads violated its spirit, or at least what it felt the injunction's spirit should be. In any event, SRF asked the court to hold Ananda in contempt.

At the same time SRF sought "clarification" from the judge that his injunction also prohibited Ananda from using Yogananda's name in any flyer, advertisement, or other public document. And for good measure, SRF asked Garcia for "minor modifications" to the injunction to prohibit use of (1) Yogananda's photo in close proximity to Ananda's name, (2) SRF's copyrighted works, and (3) sound recordings of Yogananda. These were far from minor changes, and amounted to a sweeping new injunction, including copyright relief already denied in the original motion. Garcia thought so too, and chided SRF's lawyers that the changes were more significant than they claimed. He denied both the requests to clarify and to modify the injunction. Perhaps the tide was turning.

SRF's attempt to expand the injunction also appeared to be a "message motion" to punish Kriyananda for his recent publication of *The Essence of Self-Realization*, and to discourage any such future publications. *The Essence* recorded Kriyananda's account of discussions he and others had had with Yogananda concerning Self-realization. Not only did the book display Kriyananda's close personal relationship with his Master, it highlighted Yogananda's generic use of the term "Self-realization." Clearly Kriyananda had not come to heel, and SRF needed to yank his chain. SRF had reason to worry. *The Essence of Self-Realization* has become an important source of Yogananda's teachings, revealing his wisdom and humor in new light.

During the month we waited for the hearing on the expanded injunction Ananda's religious future again hung in the balance. At the September 12, 1991 hearing, Garcia announced he was denying most of SRF's application and its request for an order of contempt. He took under submission, however, to be decided later, the part of the motion in which SRF requested an injunction on Ananda's use of certain copyrighted materials. Then, on his own, he requested the parties provide written arguments on a new issue that concerned him: had SRF waited too long to file its lawsuit? If it had, then the injunction could be denied on that basis as well.

Before granting an injunction the court must "balance the hardships" to each side in granting or denying the injunction. If SRF had failed to act promptly, and stood around for too long while Ananda infringed its rights, the judge could conclude that SRF did not really need immediate relief, and therefore did not need a preliminary injunction. "Laches" is the law's name for the concept of "you snooze you lose." Or as the California Civil Code colorfully observes, "The law protects the vigilant, before those who sleep on their rights." We appreciated Garcia voicing his concerns, and were happy to confirm them. SRF saw things differently.

Garcia did not issue his order on the expanded injunction until Valentine's Day of 1992. His long-awaited ruling denied SRF's request for expanded protections without ever reaching the question of laches. All that subsequent briefing had been whistling in the wind, but having won the motion, we did not begrudge the extra work.

SRF threw countless amounts of time and money into the case. It all seemed so foreign to the Yogananda that Ananda was telling me about. But things work at many levels, and we turned to discovering what Yogananda would have wanted to happen with his writings, his property, and his mission. What was going on around Yogananda when he wrote, spoke, or acted a certain way, all those years ago? Who was Yogananda, and how could we someday explain such a guru-preceptor to a jury off the streets of Sacramento? We knew the real story had little to do with the Yogananda you read about in the current edition of the *Autobiography*. As we went about reclaiming the history of Yogananda, there were times when those past events seemed to resonate with our current struggle, as if Kriyananda now walked in steps Yogananda had first trod decades before. The two men struggled with similar problems, and Kriyananda now faced challenges identical to those his Master had overcome.

Yogananda returned in triumph to India in 1935, after 15 years abroad. But on the eve of leaving, with everything else that needed to be done for the extended trip, Yogananda had been sued. By his closest

friend. Since their early days in India, Basu Bagchi had been Yoganan-
da's friend, disciple, and right-hand man. Yogananda had ordained
him and bestowed upon him the monastic name of Swami Dhiranan-
da. When Yogananda left India in 1920 to begin his mission in Amer-
ica, Dhirananda remained behind in Calcutta and published the first
edition of The Science of Religion. *In 1922 Yogananda called Dhi-*
rananda from India to help out in Boston, and after acquiring Mt.
Washington in 1925, Yogananda placed his trusted friend in charge of
the Los Angeles headquarters while Yogananda lectured back East.

Suddenly, in April 1929, Dhirananda showed up unannounced at
Yogananda's apartment in New York, talked Yogananda into signing
an $8,000 IOU, and returned immediately to Mt. Washington. He
packed his bags, and within days had left the organization for good.
After teaching briefly in Los Angeles, Dhirananda attended the Uni-
versity of Iowa, obtained a Ph.D., and went on to become Doctor
Basu Bagchi, Professor of Electroencephalography at the University of
Michigan.

On May 3, 1935, Dr. Bagchi filed suit against Yogananda in the
Los Angeles Superior Court to collect on the 1929 note. The press
picked up on the filing, and had a field day reporting how the process
servers were on the prowl for one of the country's most famous lectur-
ers. Yogananda had asked a patron for money to make the India trip
earlier but it did not work out, and now everyone kept the travel plans
secret. But Yogananda did not live a secret life, and they served him
before he could get out of town.

Yogananda knew the suit was coming, and on March 29, 1935,
had filed papers incorporating the Self-Realization Fellowship Church,
Inc. as a non-profit California corporation. A couple weeks after be-
ing served with the lawsuit, Yogananda signed a General Assignment
giving the new corporation all of his personal property located at Mt.
Washington. That same day he signed a Last Will and Testament. His
personal property now belonged to the church, and his will would take
care of both his U.S. and Indian organizations upon his passing. Now
no one could touch the assets that had been assembled over the years.

Three days later he gave his sworn deposition in the case, and was soon aboard a train to New York, leaving behind the lawsuit he would lose in absentia. He was headed back home to India, and not certain when, or if, he would return. For a moment the movement hung in the balance.

Chapter 4

ANANDA RESPONDS
November 1990

With new energy and greater numbers, we rebounded quickly from the initial setback. Sheila was now on board, with a keen mind and indefatigable energy that would make all the difference. And a group had galvanized around us. I have always been impressed with the caliber of intelligent and hard-working people that Ananda attracts. The community operates by consensus, made clear to me in the way the community handled the lawsuit. The "legal team" now expanded into three tiers. There was a small group of close disciples who, together with Kriyananda, reviewed all events, discussed game plans, and made the decisions, usually following consultation with Sheila and myself. There was also a core group of workers, including Sheila, Cathy, Keshava, and I, who did the heavy legal lifting: preparing and responding to the motions, drafting and reviewing discovery, and otherwise pushing the juggernaut of federal litigation. We were assisted as need arose by a seemingly endless throng of members and supporters who contributed endless hours of time, often late into the night, copying, compiling, and delivering materials. Every one played an important role.

Ananda Village / 1990

Back in the 1960s Kriyananda had joined with poets Allen Ginsberg and Gary Snyder to purchase 72 acres of land located in the northern reaches of the Sierra Nevada gold country. For Kriyananda it was a bold

43

first step to establish a spiritual community, a World Brotherhood Community, based on Yogananda's teachings. But once he bought the land, the mortgage had to be paid, and Kriyananda had to continue traveling on the road, to attract students and raise funds.

Swami Yogananda left Boston in November 1923 and headed west from Philadelphia that next July. A month later found him lecturing in Denver. By early September he was giving classes in Seattle. After a three-week cruise to Alaska he started down the coast, and by January 1925 had settled in Los Angeles. He soon found the ideal property for an international headquarters; the old Mt. Washington Hotel sitting 980 feet above Los Angeles and offering breathtaking views from the mountains to the sea. The hotel was only fifteen years old, but had fallen on hard times. Yogananda put together the right team, and within months dedicated the hotel and some surrounding parcels as the Mount Washington Educational Estates.

The property was heavily mortgaged. To pay for the purchase and the operation of the ashram, Yogananda immediately set off on the first of many lecture "campaigns" to attract students and raise funds. This non-stop circuit from city to city kept Yogananda so busy back East that he did not spend a Christmas at Mt. Washington until 1929. During those years the membership would receive a series of pleas for assistance as each loan payment came due. Many times the loan verged on default and foreclosure, but Yogananda always managed to make things happen.

Kriyananda could make things happen. By virtue of his personal energy, lectures, and fundraising, Ananda was able to put down roots and grow. Before setting eyes on Ananda Village, I had read about it. The Ananda Community consists largely of individuals, couples, and small families who live a simple life of "plain living and high thinking." At first the community members lived in tents, tepees, and yurts. These gave way to geodesic domes, and then to more conventional, but still owner-built, lathe and plaster construction. During these years, Ananda came to be recognized as an exemplar of "intentional communities." It was the subject of both scholarly and popular books, perhaps the most famous being *Ananda: Where Yoga Lives* by John Ball, the award-winning author of *In the Heat of the Night.* A disastrous forest fire in 1976 destroyed most of the residences and other buildings that had been constructed with such loving sweat. This catastrophe weeded out the less committed, and the community that remained grew back stronger and more vibrant. It was one of the first crises that helped define what Ananda was to become. Although negligence by a Nevada County employee using county equipment caused the fire, and several other landowners had obtained settlements to cover their damages, Ananda decided on principle not to take the county's money. Something different was happening here.

From the beginning Ananda was a protean idea, changing with the times and with Kriyananda's evolving understanding of his mission. From 1967–69 the property consisted of only seventy-five undeveloped acres, now called the Meditation Retreat. In those days the hills around Ananda attracted a wide variety of people seeking alternative lifestyles. Most were more tolerant than religious, and Kriyananda himself attracted both the curious and the committed. A few described the connections they felt with him in terms of past lives. Some looked for a teacher, a life's guide, or a source of insight for their own journey. In the beginning this commune community was nothing like the Village I saw in 1990. And Kriyananda was often on the road in those early years, making the dream happen.

His lectures brought in more than money. Attending one of Kriyananda's first series of classes in San Francisco in 1967, John ("Jyotish") Novak learned how to meditate. He soon approached Kriyananda and offered to be his personal assistant. Jyotish and his wife, Devi, now head Ananda Sangha Worldwide, the international teaching ministry of Ananda. The story of Ananda in those early days is the collective experience of the individuals who lived it. It changed as they did. And each person related to Kriyananda as suited them at that time. There were no house rules to follow, no regimented roles with a resulting set of duties and expectations. Kriyananda himself changed over the years as more came to be needed and expected of him, and by 1990 he was the pillar of the Ananda community. Something different was happening all the time. Now that included the lawsuit.

Discovery / 1990–2002

"Discovery" is a word that packs a lot of meaning. It refers to the exchange of information by which the parties find out what evidence the other side has, prepare their case for trial, and evaluate the pros and cons of settlement. It includes written questions to the other side ("interrogatories"), requests for copies of documents or the right to examine them ("requests for documents"), requests that the other side agree that certain facts are true ("requests for admissions"), and the opportunity to ask witnesses questions under oath, in a live session across a table ("depositions"). Each form of discovery has its use, but depositions provide a unique opportunity to get answers from a witness' mouth, while watching how the witness responds. Before we went to trial in 2002, each of the parties would take hundreds of hours of testimony in depositions north and south, coast to coast.

Discovery has become the tail wagging the litigation dog. Many lawyers who fancy themselves trial lawyers never actually go to trial, but earn princely sums conducting discovery. It is the bread-and-butter of large firms. Even cases that settle long before trial can generate hundreds of thousands of dollars gathering information that is never used. For discovery is not limited to the issues actually involved in the lawsuit. It includes information that might lead to the discovery of admissible evidence, or that might shine light on claims not yet made, but which could be made in the case. Some believe that only by getting more information than you can possibly use will you be sure to get everything you need.

Not surprisingly, discovery often exhausts the parties mentally and financially. Sometimes a wealthy litigant uses discovery to drain the limited resources of its soon-to-be penurious opponent, forcing them by economic imperative into settlement. SRF had a lot of money and a lot of lawyers. By the end of the case, SRF was on its fifth law firm.

Ananda and SRF each produced thousands of documents during the lawsuit. Hundreds of pages of original typescripts were made available in Los Angeles for review only by Ananda's counsel, and hundreds more provided at SRF's Richmond Temple for review by the litigation team just before trial. Scores of potential witnesses were interviewed, and more than a hundred ended up being used either for live testimony or by means of written declarations. Most of the leading religious experts in the field were retained by one side or the other for testimony or advice. Kriyananda and Daya Mata gave days of depositions, as did Ananda Mata, Mrinalini Mata, Uma Mata, several SRF monks, the Ananda legal team, and numerous SRF and Ananda members.

Although Kriyananda had been with Yogananda for years, served as head of the monks, and was an officer and director of SRF, much was hidden from him. In the mid-1950s, after Yogananda's passing, SRF grew increasingly secretive about him, his history, his personality, and his relationship with the organization he founded. We were able to piece together through discovery, however, the fuller picture of how Yogananda handled his copyrights and other property ownership. Yogananda paid close attention to his legal rights in the early years, but later let the details slip into the hands of others. After Yogananda returned from India in 1936 various staff members handled the copyright paperwork, and Yogananda left the mechanics of the magazine to its editors. Yogananda's inattention to some of these subtleties, combined with SRF's possession of his tangible property, provided the backbone of SRF's claims in the lawsuit.

Most of SRF's claims in the lawsuit can be summed up in SRF's assertion that Yogananda had given everything to SRF: his physical assets, his intangible rights, and even his personal attributes such as his name, voice, and likeness. SRF even claimed that in 1935 Yogananda gave SRF the exclusive right to use Yogananda's name, voice, signature, photograph, and likeness—even though these forms of property interests would not be recognized by the California legislature for another thirty years. Many of SRF's similarly broad assertions were inherently suspect. But each had to be investigated and disproved. We hoped that discovery would allow us to put the lie to these bold but baseless claims.

Paramhansa Yogananda arrived at the Biltmore Hotel in downtown Los Angeles on the evening of March 7, 1952, keynote speaker at a dinner welcoming Indian Ambassador Binay R. Sen to Los Angeles. Moments before taking the dais on stage to join the honored guests and other speakers, he paused before the lobby fountain to allow Arthur Say of the Los Angeles Times *to take a few photos for inclusion in the next day's newspaper account. As Yogananda concluded his talk with the poem "My India," to the shock and dismay of the onlooking guests he slipped to the floor of the stage in his* mahasamadhi, *a yogi's final conscious exit from his body. When Yogananda did not return to Mt. Washington and no one else showed up to demand his things, SRF kept them. The longer SRF held on to Yogananda's property, the more guardianship felt like ownership. Possession is, after all, nine points of the law.*

Gurus in the Hindu tradition typically have many followers, some of whom become swamis in their own right and found their own ashrams. These branches typically co-exist in peace, and cooperate during festivals and other religious events. Life teachings are passed along by personal instruction from teacher to student through the guru-disciple relationship. Given this long-standing historical tradition, it would have been alien to Yogananda's line of gurus to trust his mission to a single follower. Entrusting it to a lifeless corporation would accordingly be unthinkable. Yogananda acknowledged that his guru's guru had "steadfastly refused to permit his followers to build any organization around the teachings." Could

Yogananda have changed so much? It appears he did not, and that Yogananda did not see SRF as the sole and final expression of his life's work.

During Yogananda's lifetime his mission generated a separate organization that flourished in Washington, D.C. Yogananda had set up Brahmachari Jotin as the head of the Washington Yogoda Center in June 1928. He was so successful that his church adopted a separate identity, and name, as the Church of Absolute Monism. Yogananda encouraged and spoke favorably about this organization, and in July 1941 gave Jotin his monastic vows and the name Swami Premananda.

We also found that during Yogananda's life many of the teachers affiliated with him were running virtually autonomous operations in distant cities. Others, such as Hamid Bey and Roman Ostoja, were associated with Yogananda for a number of years and then spun off on their own. Hamid Bey, for example, went on to found the Coptic Fellowship. The organization known as Yogoda Sat-Sanga in the 1920s, and the Self-Realization Fellowship of the early 1930s, was a vibrant organization in constant flux. The reality of Yogananda's existence in those days, and his relationship with SRF, differed much from the story SRF was now telling about a monolithic and regimented organization controlling the guru who founded it.

Yogananda had also encouraged "householders"—married disciples living outside the organization—to have an active role in spreading the teachings. Kamala Silva, for example, had lived with her husband in the Bay Area and remained active in local Center affairs. Dr. Minott W. Lewis, Yogananda's "first American *kriyaban*" was married, as was James J. "Saint" Lynn, the second president of SRF who Yogananda renamed Rajarshi Janakananda. Even Yogananda's guru, Sri Yukteswar, was married, as was *his* guru, Lahiri Mahasaya. Celibacy was not a big deal until SRF made it one.

After Sister Daya was elected president in 1955, several male disciples left SRF to found their own communities: Roy Eugene Davis (Center for Spiritual Awareness in Lakemont, Georgia), Norman Paulsen (Solar Logos, now Sunburst in Buellton, California), Bob Raymer, and of course, Kriyananda. In addition, J. Oliver Black, a close disciple and dynamic center leader who had never lived at SRF, founded Song of the Morning Retreat Center, near Vanderbilt, Michigan. It was all part of the natural growth of Yogananda's legacy, which he never intended to be expressed through a single voice or organization.

The First Deposition / May 1992

A deposition involves a lawyer asking questions of a witness who has been placed under oath. The questions and answers are typed up in a transcript by the court reporter, and may be used later at trial in place of warm-body testimony. A deposition may last from hours to days, and we took or defended over fifty depositions in the federal case. Some, occasionally all, of the legal team attended each deposition. For years it seemed like we were always preparing for, or flying off to, one deposition after another.

"A journey of a thousand miles begins with a single step." The depositions began in Portland, Oregon, with an SRF member who had no idea of the role she played in SRF's game. Both churches enjoyed active followings in Portland. Ananda maintained a residential community with an affiliated bookstore in town, and SRF supported a meditation group, of which Ms. Carolyn McKean was a member. As part of SRF's thorough preparation of its case, she had been asked, and dutifully agreed, to give a written statement called a "declaration." The McKean declaration stated that she was confused by Ananda's use of the term "Self-realization" because SRF was also using that term. The declaration's language craftily insinuated that Ananda was pretending to be affiliated with SRF. SRF's lawyers prepared the declaration, had McKean sign it, and submitted the document with their application for a preliminary injunction. Garcia referred to the McKean declaration in his ruling, and appeared to be strongly influenced by it. If we were to undo the injunction, the McKean declaration was the place to start. On a beautiful May morning we began this new phase of the case by deposing this sweet and gentle stranger.

McKean's deposition testimony differed significantly from the carefully chosen language SRF had placed in her declaration. Written declarations are always prepared by the lawyers, so all you really know is that the declarant signed the document once it was finished and placed before her. We thought SRF had been finessing certain facts, and it was time to turn the declaration's verbiage into McKean's own words. She did not disappoint. When asked the right questions, she explained that she was not so much confused by Ananda as she was interested in it, and did not understand the differences between the two organizations. It turned out that no one had misled her or tricked her into doing anything. Her confusion was the product of a healthy curiosity, not any misrepresentation. Her deposition testimony did not support SRF's claims.

Within weeks of taking McKean's deposition we had our motion to dissolve the preliminary injunction drafted and in front of Judge Garcia. We wanted the judge to hear what McKean had to say, and how her actual words varied from the declaration SRF had given him, and upon which he had relied in granting the preliminary injunction. In his detailed June 21, 1993 order explaining his dissolution of the preliminary injunction, Garcia observed that:

> . . . The declaration of Carolyn McKean, the only evidence of actual confusion presented in support of the motion for preliminary injunction, has now been discredited by her deposition testimony.

It was not McKean, but SRF, whose testimony had been discredited. This would not be the last time that SRF's claims overreached its facts. McKean had begun to open Garcia's eyes.

A Protective Order / May 1992

It is typical for parties to enter into some form of confidentiality agreement, called a "Protective Order," concerning the documents produced in discovery. It is generally a good idea to prevent the disclosure of trade secrets and leakage of sensitive business or personal information outside the lawsuit. The usual terms provide that when confidential documents are produced, they are conspicuously marked "Confidential." The receiving parties and their attorney are then obligated to keep those documents confidential. Their restricted use is often detailed in the order, and when the lawsuit ends the documents are returned.

We assumed that SRF would assert confidentiality concerning personnel matters, financial data, and information about the inner workings of the board of directors. But SRF had a more embracing vision of confidentiality. Everything—literally everything—about SRF produced in the lawsuit was confidential, including its history, writings, and teachings. SRF claimed that every fact it disclosed about Yogananda's life was confidential. SRF's proposed confidentiality order created two tiers of confidentiality. The most confidential tier, "Highly Restricted Confidential Matter," consisted of documents which could only be seen by counsel and a single representative of the parties. This ultra-secret "Highly Restricted" material consisted of "Doctrinal and theological information" and "information, not now publicly available, regarding the history of the parties or the life of Paramahansa Yogananda." SRF might have to disclose the truth in the lawsuit, but the world would know only SRF's manicured version of Yogananda's life, a reverent biography that no longer reflected Yogananda's electric vitality and the exuberance that drew people to him. It was a protective order, all right, protecting SRF's assumed persona.

SRF understood that maintaining its story of who Yogananda was, and what his mission meant, depended on keeping its trove of records and writings secret. For example, Yogananda completed his work explaining the Bhagavad Gita the year before his passing. In 1951 he wrote to Rajarshi that he had received the galley sheets for "Spiritual Interpretation of the Bhagavad Gita," and that he expected the book out in print any day. The demands of other tasks prevented its publication during Yogananda's lifetime, but SRF then sat on the publication for another 40 years while Mrinalini Mata claimed to be toiling away on it "day and night." SRF only published its bowdlerized edition of the work during the lawsuit, after Kriyananda threatened to release his own version. Like so many other writings, SRF released its publication as containing the "pure" writings, even though they were the product of years of heavy-handed editing. SRF could not assert purity with impunity if the public had copies of what Yogananda really wrote. SRF needed a protective order.

We tried to negotiate a reduced scope for SRF's proposed order, but the day before McKean's deposition, the court granted SRF's request for a Protective Order in the form proposed by SRF. This order of the court from 1992, modified slightly in 2001, governs the confidential information disclosed during the lawsuit. It remains binding on the parties and their lawyers to the present. Because of this Protective Order, the copies of Yogananda's original writings and talks that we received during the lawsuit could not be made public, and were given back to SRF at the end of the case. Much that was learned must remain unmentioned. Some of the key documents in the case nonetheless slipped into the public's eye during the appeals, such as Yogananda's two wills and the 1935 General Assignment Yogananda signed before leaving for India. SRF made some documents public at the time and others have turned up in private collections or on the open market. I am able to write this memoir today only because the lawsuit led me to other sources, and to people familiar with SRF, who shared their experiences and documents. The truth is out there and publicly available, but still hard to find.

First Fruits / 1991–1992

Although they delayed, dissembled, and held back, SRF ultimately produced a wealth of original documents for our review. There was something special in holding those old original documents—the correspondence, the early editions of works, the fading papers of typescript—that gave the case an immediacy, a deeper reality, and a feel for the person behind the words. In college I enjoyed researching through dusty archives, finding original sources weathered with age. One of the best parts of this adventure was holding and reading the original materials written, or read, by Yogananda himself. These included tax returns from the earliest days, private letters, and confidential memos and manuscripts in Yogananda's own hand. It was as if we stood reading over the Master's shoulder, or listening to the flow of his accented English. The typescripts of his early talks, many bearing the initials "fw" for Faye Wright, seemed to carry still something of the energy that flowed from Yogananda in those days. And these many writings, transcriptions, and recordings were only a small part of SRF's hidden treasures.

Every document told us something new, and hinted what we should ask for next. The more SRF dug in its heels and refused to produce documents, the more we knew we were getting close to something good. Slowly, over the years, we peeled back layers of information from SRF's documents, cooperative third parties, and public records. Yogananda began to emerge again as a charismatic and dynamic leader of SRF, and of other organizations. It was becoming clear that SRF's current argument about the role of SRF in Yogananda's mission contained more wishful thinking than fact. People were drawn to Yogananda, not to the corporation.

Yogananda made an impression. He was just 5' 5" tall, with a stocky build, but he filled the room with his presence. Many people recorded their impressions of first meeting, seeing, or hearing him. M.R. Keith wrote how in the audience he "sensed a great wave of power flowing down from Yogananda, who was standing over me. A great scintillating light appeared and ... [a] feeling of utter and absolute peace and well being filled me with ecstasy." Kamala Silva, then still a teenager, attended Yogananda's first Los Angeles lecture in January 1925, and wrote in her diary that "His smile is like the sunshine of a soul." Over the next several weeks he lectured or taught almost every night, and Kamala reported "his words possessed an oratory of a kind to rouse the listener from spiritual slumber."

And the Swami could put on a show, long raven locks cascading down his shoulders and over his orange robe. There would often be some musical entertainment, and Yogananda would typically perform one or more feats of wonder, including stopping his heart, doing effort-

less headstands, or conducting faith healings. There would be oppor-
tunities for the audience to come on stage and participate, and doctors
to verify that he could make his pulse beat differently in his right and
left arms. During the Depression years he toured with a troupe that
sometimes seemed more vaudeville than spiritual. Hamid Bey's spe-
cialty was being buried alive, and "Count" Roman Ostoja would stick
needles through his tongue and skin.

Yogananda was a spellbinding orator. In strongly accented but flu-
ent English he would wax poetic, then practical, about Yogoda: his
blend of meditation, exercise, yoga, and positive thinking designed for
the man on the street. It was a "practical philosophy" that everyone
could use to advantage, regardless of religious belief. He told business-
men how to recharge their cosmic business batteries and women how
to find their spiritual mates. Striding back and forth across the stage,
he would come to a stop and stand talking where the overhead spot
crowned him with a nimbus of light. America was ready for Yogoda.
Celebrities and socialites signed on to tout the benefits of Yogoda and
have their picture taken with the Swami. Wherever he went, photos
and stories appeared in the press. He was a bona fide phenomenon.

Yogananda's Wills / 1993

In the sadness and ceremony of Yogananda's sudden passing there was
no mention of any will. As heirs and devotees grieved and carried on, no
one mentioned any will. But Yogananda had left a will. He had left two
wills. One had been signed in 1935 before he left for India, and a second
in 1936 while he was back in Calcutta. During the lawsuit SRF first denied there was any will, but eventually had to produce both of them, and
then explain why they had not been disclosed sooner. And to this day
SRF has never been called to task by Yogananda's heirs who might have
been denied their rights under those wills.

SRF claimed that during Yogananda's lifetime he gave it everything he owned, lock, stock, and barrel. Therefore, as SRF first posited, there was no will because there was no need for one. "Why would Yogananda need a will?" Daya Mata once asked. But when the wills turned up, they showed that Yogananda had carefully considered which organizations were to receive what portion of his estate, and SRF was not the sole object of his affection. Daya and Ananda Mata did their best to forget about the wills. It was only after losing a key motion, when further silence risked greater loss, that Ananda Mata allegedly stumbled across the first will in the basement vault. She and her sister had both been close to Yogananda at the time the wills were made, and must have known about them. But Ananda Mata blustered about her shock and surprise to now discover such an important document. When weeks later SRF's growing need precipitated Ananda Mata's discovery of a *second* forgotten will, her credibility took further lumps. Good things come in threes they say, and I have always wondered what a thorough search of the vault would reveal.

The wills became key pieces of evidence. They showed that Yogananda thought he would own property at the time of his death, that he had actively arranged for the disposition of that property, and that SRF should have received only part of Yogananda's estate. In addition, there was a "residue" from the wills that should have gone to Yogananda's heirs, including perhaps his intangible rights. But no one told the heirs about the wills or their effect, and the heirs never claimed their due. Ananda Mata's dissembling in her declarations so badly damaged her credibility that Garcia made a big deal about refusing to consider what she said in her declarations.

The "K File" / 1993

Word had long swirled down from Mt. Washington that intelligence about Kriyananda went straight to the office of the president, where Daya Mata and her sister would review it and then place it in a special "K File" they kept in the president's outer office. The rumors proved true. Officially, SRF did not care what Kriyananda did. Privately SRF tracked his every move and obsessed over every writing. The leadership read everything he wrote. Copies of Kriyananda's books that SRF produced in discovery were annotated throughout by monks and nuns who commented on everything from subject matter to grammatical style.

I had read Kriyananda's autobiography, called *The Path,* accounting his own attraction to Yogananda, his years living with his Master at SRF, and his journey onward to the Ananda Community. It was based on, and a homage to, Yogananda's own principal work, *Autobiography of a Yogi,* and told of Kriyananda's adventures through 1977. We found a copy of this book in SRF's "K File" with detailed notes and negative comments on almost every page. Kriyananda has recently issued an updated edition, called *The New Path,* and I imagine it too has been annotated and shelved somewhere on Mt. Washington.

The thick file, as it turned out, held nothing significant for the case. It looked like something a fan might have assembled about a matinee idol, with an attention to minutiae that spoke of fixation. Clearly people at the top of the company were still personally struggling with "K." The current lawsuit was just another chapter in that unfolding drama.

The Magistrate Judge / 1991–2002

Judge Garcia presided over the course of the lawsuit, but appointed a magistrate judge to hear and decide disputes concerning discovery. Magistrate judges are appointed by the local District Court judges for 14 year terms. They lack the broad judicial authority or the lifetime tenure of District Court judges. Instead, magistrate judges are employees of the court, acting as assistants to the judges and often deciding interim issues the judge doesn't want to handle. For example, the judge might refer the fact-finding part of a motion to the magistrate judge, who then issues a recommendation for the judge's action. These recommendations are typically adopted by the judge without modification. We were assigned Magistrate Judge Peter A. Nowinski.

We once challenged a Nowinski recommendation and tried to get Garcia to go with a different order. His Honor adopted the magistrate judge's proposal without change, and impressed upon us the confidence he held in his magistrate judge, in a manner telling us that any further requests would be a waste of time. Nowinski decided the many discovery motions that both sides brought seeking more documents, or more depositions, or fuller answers to questions. They all seemed very important at the time, and the discovery provided the facts upon which we built our later motions. But they added mightily to the cost.

Before a discovery motion will be heard, the parties must agree on and submit a "stipulated" set of facts, using language agreed on by both sides. While a good idea in theory, and often workable in less contentious cases, it became virtually impossible for our two sides to agree on a single statement about anything. We soon adopted a practice where each side stated its position on each issue, and we stitched the opposing arguments next to each other. The arguments were often at cross-purposes, but Nowinski got the idea.

It was not always pretty. For example, when SRF brought a motion in July 1992 to compel Ananda to provide yet further responses to yet more interrogatories, Nowinski denied it. But he also issued an "Order to Show Cause" why SRF's counsel and I should not both be held in contempt for our bellicose posturing. Counsel for the parties trekked to Sacramento, and after a sincere showing of contrite remorse for our jactitation Nowinski discharged the order to show cause and imposed no sanctions. But he sternly ordered counsel to "meet and confer" on the discovery dispute within the next twenty-one days. It was the closest we came to being officially reprimanded, but not the last time the court complained about counsels' conduct.

Peeling the Onion / 1993–1997

As we dug deeper and understood better the relationship between Yogananda and his organizations, we appreciated how SRF was spinning that history. A strategy started to emerge. To decrease the expense, delay, and uncertainty of a jury trial, we would cut the case into bite-sized pieces, and bring a series of motions to eliminate parts of the case at a time. If we could trim the case enough, surely SRF would come to the bargaining table. A peace treaty could be hammered out allowing both organizations to coexist. During those days our goal was still to encourage settlement so that everyone would walk away from the dispute with dignity.

To get the most bang for Ananda's donors' buck, we culled the complaint for its weak links. I called these its "feet of legal clay." The complaint made sweeping claims based upon broadly alleged facts. Assuming those facts were true, the complaint presented a formidable aspect. But what if we were able to show that SRF could not prove some fact that was basic to its case—like the ownership of writings in which SRF claimed copyright? For example, SRF had photographic negatives, and "original prints", of several disputed photographs. But the 1909 Copyright Act provided that the *photographer* owned the copyright in a photograph. We needed to put SRF to the test: prove who took the photos and how SRF obtained the copyright from that photographer. If SRF could not identify the photographer, SRF could not prove that it legally acquired the copyright. Without ownership there could be no claim for infringement or for damages. So a single factual weakness might bring SRF's mighty arguments tumbling down.

We needed to understand, and then educate Garcia on, one piece of the puzzle at a time. But where to begin? The first motion or motions should attack the factual assumptions of the preliminary injunction, so that favorable rulings could be folded into a follow-up motion to dissolve that injunction. The legal team played a major role in this sort of strategy decision, as well as many tactical calls along the way. These discussions were usually lively affairs with a free exchange of ideas and opinions. Kriyananda would be involved sooner or later in all important decisions, but it remained a process of consensus. It helps when you can draw from a pool of talented and motivated people, and the legal team comprised just such people. Together we focused goals and refined the approach to achieve maximum erosive effect on SRF's claims, at a pace Ananda could afford. In motion after motion, we would roll in waves to cleanse away those feet of clay. Bubbles trying to become the sea.

We did not need to win every motion, and did not expect to. Summary adjudication motions are highly technical and formalistic. They must be planned out, thoroughly researched, and supported by well-crafted arguments that make sense viscerally as well as legally. All the required evidence must be provided with the motion, presented in accordance with the Federal Rules of Evidence, and properly "authenticated" so that the judge may rely upon it. The simplest of summary adjudication motions can become major motion pictures, and our first motion was an epic—attempting nothing less than a comprehensive presentation on the use of the term "Self-realization" through millennia of practice in the Hindu-Yoga religious tradition. Why start small?

The last time I "pulled an all-nighter" was back in college. Now, many times we worked through the night to meet filing deadlines, with the final product, warts and all, rushed out the door at the last minute to make it to court in time to be filed. These were the days before electronic filings, and once Sheila and I approved the final versions of documents and signed them, they still had to be copied, assembled, served on opposing counsel by mail or overnight delivery, and filed with the court in Sacramento. The court closed at 4:30 PM, and the traffic from the Bay Area to Sacramento was unpredictable. If papers were not out the door by 1:00 PM, all bets were off that they would make it on time. Even when the exhibits were assembled beforehand, putting the final package together for filing could take hours. And there were always last minute changes that just had to be made.

We did our final joint writing and editing at Sheila's apartment in the Mountain View community. Another apartment on the other side of the complex had been set up as an office with computers, tables, supplies, and a copier. This is where the final product would be printed, proofed, copied, and collated. At these tables sat ranks of stalwart souls who put together the reams of papers that made our arguments happen. Many times I shuttled the latest version of some declaration or brief from Sheila's place to the office for printing and circulation, walking under clear starry skies in the wee hours of night. Years into the adventure, with no end I sight, I wondered how many sleepless nights would be spent before Ananda saw brighter days.

Cathy Parojinog was one of the stalwart staff who often labored through the dawn. She and I are opera fans, and our theme song those long nights became the aria from Puccini's opera Turandot, called "Nessun dorma"—"none shall sleep." Our hero in the story had won the princess' hand, but then offers to release her from that bond, and forfeit his life, if she can guess his name by dawn. Desperate for time and information, the princess commands the city to wake and help her discover his name. Was our task less meaningful, if less mortal? We worked for the world, we few, we brothers and sisters in arms. That world should wake with us.

Yogananda put in the hours. On those endless campaigns through one city after another, he seldom slept. In November 1927 he informed his audience at the Canopus Club in St. Paul that he "easily" worked 23 hours a day. There was so much to be done: interviews for the local papers, a luncheon talk, an afternoon tea, free lectures for six nights in a row, and then the Yogoda classes. Articles had to be written for the bi-monthly East-West Magazine. *He needed to generate the articles or the presses would stop, as they did when he stayed three months in Mexico. And the books continued to come out year after year, edition after edition.* Songs of the Soul, *a collection of spiritual poems, first appeared in 1923, and by 1926 was already in a fifth edition.* The Science of Religion, *his first work, went through six editions between 1920 and 1928. There were lessons for the correspondence course, new materials for the next series of classes, and the letters from devotees and supporters asking for advice and a piece of his time. Yogananda witnessed many a quiet night redden into the growl of a city waking around him.*

Chapter 5

DECONSTRUCTING SRF'S CASE

1991–1992

We decided to first file three motions, one after another, and see how Judge Garcia responded. Depending on his response, we could then fine-tune our presentation or even abandon some approaches. The first motion would challenge SRF's exclusive right to use "Self-realization" and question SRF's ownership of several specific writings. The second motion would attack SRF's state service mark of Yogananda's name, and the third its federal registration of that same mark. These last two would be ready for filing as soon as we had a response to the first. This three-step opening should permit us to strike at SRF's legal and moral claim to exclusive rights in the names "Self-Realization" and "Yogananda," and challenge its copyrights in several key works. If we won these first motions we might be in position to ask Garcia to dissolve the preliminary injunction. Our legal arguments were fairly straightforward. The evidence, on the other hand, was detailed and extensive. We wanted Garcia to begin to see the religious dimensions of the case, and Ananda's position within the Hindu-Yoga tradition. The first motion for summary adjudication on "Self-Realization" and some of the copyright issues got Garcia's attention.

"Self-Realization" Is Generic / November 1991

On November 7, 1991 Ananda filed its first motion summary adjudication motion asserting, in part, that Ananda was entitled to use "Self-Realization" in its name because that term was "generic" when used this way. It is often hard to decide whether a given mark is or is not generic, but as a general rule a generic term is a colloquial description of, or an accepted name for, some general class of product or service. A name that merely identifies the product itself is not a protectable trademark, because it does not direct the viewer's attention to the company that is the source of that product. If a mark does not function to identity the supplier of the good or service, then it does not function as a trademark and cannot be registered as one. If SRF's "Self-realization" mark was generic, then Ananda could use it for any purpose related to its generic meaning, including as part of Ananda's name.

You need to give your judge a lot of information before he can determine that a word or phrase is "generic" in a given context, which in our case meant that "Self-realization" expressed a fundamental idea in the parties' religious practices. For example, a fruit stand along the road selling apples and calling itself "The Apple Store" is using a generic name. The Apple Store is simply an apple-selling store, and you cannot stop a competitor from using that name to identify its apple-selling store. An "Apple Store" selling consumer electronics, on the other hand, would be using "apple" in a non-generic context, and therefore might be entitled to trademark protection for use with those goods. A church teaching Christian theology should never be able to obtain the exclusive right to use words like "Salvation" or "Born Again" in its name. These words state the ultimate goal of its religious practice, such that all churches within that religious tradition should be able to use those words to name themselves and signal their participation in that tradition. We thought "Self-realization" was similarly generic when used as a name by a church that taught Self-realization as the path to union with God. Now we only had to convince Garcia.

To obtain the evidence to support this motion, the team obtained statements from spiritual leaders around the world. Uses of the phrase were culled from ancient religious works, modern lectures, respected treatises, and most importantly, from Yogananda's and SRF's own writings. It was a tremendous undertaking that required reading hundreds of articles, books, and internet materials for appropriate quotes. Each work was then copied in pertinent part, highlighted, digested, and included in the growing compendium.

It's hard to know ahead of time just when you have assembled enough evidence to prove that a term like "self-realization" is generic. So we put together 2,445 pages of exhibits and sixteen declarations from leaders of many schools and religious organizations from around the world, all of whom sought or taught "self-realization." The paperwork became so voluminous that we obtained permission to file the documents in three-ring binders and ended up submitting twelve three-inch binders stuffed with exhibits.

SRF's Phantom Copyrights / November 1991

This first motion did double duty. In addition to the trademark argument, it asserted that SRF lacked any valid copyright in certain Yogananda works for which it was claiming trademark infringement damages. I liked the idea that we were "carrying the war into Africa," like old-time tacticians. We would defend by attacking. At first it had been difficult coming to grips with SRF's hydra-headed copyright claims. Everything Ananda published involved some Yogananda quote, photo, or vignette from his life. The infringements supposedly included books, talks, and articles in the magazines, as well as unpublished manuscripts. Each type of use was governed by its own set of federal or state laws. Some works were first published before Yogananda's passing, some afterwards, and some not at all. Each group presented its own set of issues.

The 1909 Copyright Act gave us the handle we needed. The Act divided copyright protection into two separate back-to-back periods called the "initial term" and the "renewal term." The initial term of copyright was for twenty-eight years from date of first publication. The copyright would then expire, unless it was properly continued for a "renewal term" of another twenty-eight years. Under the Act, the author of a writing was assumed to hold the copyright. If he died during the initial twenty-eight-year term, only a small and clearly defined group of people could renew the copyright for the second term. If there was no next of kin and no executor, then only the following people could renew: (1) the employer of a "work for hire"; (2) the assignee of a "posthumous work";

(3) the "proprietor" of a "periodical, encyclopedic, and composite" work; and (4) the "corporate body" that copyrighted the work "other than as an assignee or licensee" of the author. Unless one of these people filed a timely renewal, the copyright would lapse into the public domain. It presented a fistful of thorny terms, many whose meanings were far from clear.

Sheila and I decided to start with a manageable set of works—books that had been copyrighted by Yogananda himself, and then renewed by SRF after his passing. At the time of his *mahasamadhi* in March 1952, some of Yogananda's copyrights were still in their initial term. When those initial terms were about to expire SRF renewed the copyrights by claiming it was one of the persons permitted by the Act to do so. The stated reason would change—sometimes SRF claimed it was Yogananda's employer that had obtained the copyright as a "work for hire." Other times SRF claimed the work had actually been written by SRF itself as a "corporate body." Turns out no one at the Copyright Office ever looked into these varying claims, or asked for any proof. So for decades after 1952, SRF renewed Yogananda's copyrights in its own name, claiming it owned the underlying copyright for whatever reason sounded good at the time. The heirs never complained and no one called SRF's bluff. Until now. Until Ananda forced SRF to show its hand. And if SRF was bluffing Ananda could possibly win everything, be awarded its fees, and free up a body of Yogananda's writings for the world.

We had asked for documents on these ownership issues in discovery, but assumed that SRF was holding back on us. What we had from discovery and our own digging showed that SRF lacked copyrights in at least this first narrowly defined group of books. SRF had shown nothing to indicate it was one of the people authorized by the 1909 Act to renew copyrights first taken in Yogananda's name. We could not tell, however, whether SRF was hiding the ball or really empty-handed.

As mentioned, we used that special form of motion called "summary adjudication" to reach these issues. When the important facts are not in dispute, and the legal consequences of those facts are clear, a judge can summarily adjudicate claims without the need for a trial. We thought this procedure might incidentally provide a form of "clean up" discovery. Federal law on summary adjudication provided for a shifting burden of proof as part of the motion process. Once our opening papers showed that SRF appeared to lack evidence to prove a claim, SRF had to come forward with sufficient evidence to show that it *might* be able to win that claim at trial. The legal team figured that a serious motion for summary adjudication would scare SRF into disclosing all it had, or risk losing the claim through ignoble inaction. There were risks. We never knew what evidence SRF might be withholding, and we would need to disclose our best arguments, only to lose if SRF produced new evidence. But even if we lost the motion we could renew our arguments at trial, and we would see SRF's best evidence before that showdown.

The legal team often discussed how whatever Ananda placed in the public domain would benefit the world. At the time Ananda was the only group sufficiently strong and organized to challenge SRF's claimed monopoly on the teachings. People at Ananda began to refer to our efforts in terms of "Master for the World." Yet the direct conflict with SRF left many in the community uncomfortable and confused about how to respond. It was one thing to read about some mythic battle like that recounted in the Bhagavad Gita, and something else to live the struggle at home. Some found comfort and direction by focusing on making the works available as Yogananda wrote them. Some threw themselves into the effort itself. I found comfort in the past.

Yogananda acquired Mt. Washington in October 1925, but not without controversy. Arriving in town on January 2, Yogananda soon found the ideal spot to base his work. The old hotel near the top of Mt. Washington was available, though run-down and filled with vagrants. The tram that took movie stars up to the hotel during its brief heyday would never work again, but private automobiles were becoming the rage. Yogananda put together a team to handle what he called "the detailed legal end of acquiring the property" that included prominent

attorney and former Representative James McLachlan, as well as local bigwigs W.C. Bramham and P. Rogers.

Their connections soon had the ball rolling, and Yogananda was so eager that he conducted an Easter Service on the property before the papers were even finalized. The team incorporated a new holding company, arranged financing, and through a series of sometimes-secret sales, acquired several parcels around the hotel. Repairs were commenced and the premises readied for a gala dedication to be conducted Sunday, October 25, 1925. Announcements touted the many politicians and socialites of Roaring Twenties Los Angeles who were expected to attend.

Two weeks before the dedication, one of the sellers sued. Emma Mitchell filed suit in the Los Angeles Superior Court on October 13, 1925, accusing Swami Giri Yogananda of fraud in the acquisition of her parcel. She alleged that certain statements had been made that induced her to sell, that those statements turned out to be false, and that she was now entitled to damages and the return of her property. This could become a serious problem if other sellers starting crying foul. Title to some parcels had been taken in the name of straw men, including family members of the team, and it could prove embarrassing.

Others closer to home were also complaining. The Thursday before Sunday's dedication Capt. M. Rashid, Yogananda's road manager for his talks and classes, filed suit alleging that he was entitled to twenty-five percent of the "net proceeds of all lectures, fees, contributions or other monies received" by Yogananda. If there was money to buy a hotel, Rashid figured there was money to pay him. The news grew worse Friday, when Rashid obtained a writ of attachment and levied on two of Yogananda's bank accounts. On the eve of the opening Yogananda's funds were frozen.

The dedication went off Sunday, October 25, without a hitch. The next day Yogananda came to an understanding with Rashid, who dismissed his lawsuit. The Mitchell case dragged on for three months as the parties wrangled, but it too settled. On January 22, 1926, Mitchell dismissed her case without public explanation. Even masters on the path have to deal with conflict and uncertainty.

Ananda Wins a Big One / April 1992

On the morning of April 24, 1992, we stood again before Garcia. He had developed a standard practice for our hearings, which began by asking counsel if there was anything they wanted to add to their already voluminous papers. The paperwork was usually so thorough that it was hard to imagine that anything could have been overlooked or now needed to be added. But SRF's lead counsel at the time would sometimes hold up a copy of an appellate decision "newly issued" or "just discovered" that he was sure would persuade Garcia that Ananda must lose that day's motion. Garcia patiently listened to whatever we said, thanked us for being as brief as we could, and then read his decision from the detailed longhand notes he had already written. The man thought his positions through, with clearly stated reasons, and was not likely to be dissuaded by some last minute observation. The typical motion thus proceeded with the lawyers "submitting" the matter on the papers, and then trying to follow Garcia's long detailed analysis, taking notes for any needed comments. Garcia would sometimes quiz us at the end, if he wanted to be sure we understood him. Garcia always gave us an opportunity to argue after receiving his wisdom, and sometimes we couldn't stop ourselves from talking, but I never recall him changing a ruling on the fly.

In this way we heard the good news that reversed the case's direction. Garcia began his ruling by agreeing with Ananda that the way both parties used the term "Self-realization" was generic. Yes! Exactly what we had hoped for. Now where would he go with this? How many dominoes would fall? He then abruptly "continued" the rest of the hearing to a later date, including the motion on the service mark and our request to dissolve the preliminary injunction. He told us he hadn't decided these issues yet because of the overwhelming volume of paperwork, and we would have to wait for him to read it all. It took two more months, but it was worth the wait.

Reciprocating Motions / May 1992

SRF never gave up. A month after Garcia's oral ruling, and a month before we got his final order, SRF filed a motion asking Garcia to "reconsider" whether Self-realization was a generic term, at least to the extent that SRF used the term as a mark to sell its goods and services. That same day, Ananda reciprocated by filing its second summary adjudication motion, the one challenging the alleged "Paramahansa Yogananda" service mark under California law. In addition, encouraged by Garcia's first ruling, we began preparing the motion to dissolve the preliminary injunction. Rather than waiting upon our hoped-for decisions, we filed it as soon as we could, and asked Garcia to dissolve the injunction at the same time he invalidated the state and federal service marks.

SRF asked Garcia to take another look at his "Self-realization" ruling, claiming that even if the term was generic in SRF's name, SRF also used the term as a mark to sell its goods and services. When used in connection with those goods and services, SRF argued, the term "Self-realization" was "descriptive" rather than "generic." In other words, when used to advertise classes, retreats, and books, "Self-realization" described the subject matter of those goods and services, rather than indicating an ultimate religious objective. Subtle, but significant. If the mark was merely descriptive, then a different test would apply, and SRF could keep its ownership by showing that the mark had achieved something called "secondary meaning."

Secondary meaning is another term of art, referring to the way the public gradually comes to associate a common descriptive word with a specific supplier. The mark "Windows," for example, describes the Microsoft computer program that operates by means of a series of sizable windows that the user can enlarge, minimize, and move around. For years the Trademark Office rejected Microsoft's efforts to register the Windows mark because the mark was merely descriptive, and Microsoft had not yet shown the required secondary meaning. After billions spent in advertising, sales, and interviews, the company finally produced public surveys and expert opinions saying that when prospective purchasers *saw* the word "Windows" on a software application they *thought* of Microsoft. That showing of secondary meaning—the public's mental connection between a descriptive mark and a specific supplier—permitted Microsoft to finally register the Windows mark. SRF's new motion did not challenge our victory concerning the church's name, but raised troubling questions about the ruling's application to goods and services, and threatened to overshadow what we had won.

Indeed, if Garcia decided that SRF's marketing use of "Self-Realization" was merely descriptive and might had acquired secondary meaning, then Ananda would lose that portion of the motion unless our showing had incidentally negated that secondary meaning. The concern was that our presentation back then had not focused on negating secondary meaning. We had addressed it, but only in passing as a second-tier issue. Further arguments and additional facts could have been provided, and now this major ruling rested on whether our evidence would prove more than we had originally offered it for.

Yogananda Is No Service Mark / May–September 1992

We filed our motion challenging the California registration of "Paramahansa Yogananda" on May 29, 1992, and four months later followed up with the companion motion attacking the federal service mark registration. SRF claimed that "Paramahansa Yogananda" was both a state and a federal service mark, and had officially registered it as such. A service mark is a word or image that consumers use to identify the provider of some desired service, like "Midas" for mufflers or "H&R Block" for taxes. A protectable mark must be used in a trademark manner—to identify the supplier. SRF used Yogananda's name, however, only to refer to that person who was Yogananda, what he did, said, or thought. SRF's own writings often used the phrase "Paramahansa Yogananda, Founder" indicating they were talking about the person who founded SRF. SRF never used its guru's name to identify itself as the purveyor of any "Paramahansa Yogananda"-branded services. We also pointed out that SRF actually used other marks to identify itself, namely the three letters "SRF" and its fuller "Self-Realization Fellowship" name. It seemed so clear to us, but it was Garcia's opinion that mattered.

Along the way we noted (or rubbed in) how the spelling "Paramahansa" was actually a corruption of the title that Yogananda himself used. It was another example of SRF playing around with the past and reconfiguring Yogananda to meet its needs. In the summer of 1958, after Sister Daya's trip to India, SRF suddenly changed the spelling of Yogananda's title from "Paramhansa" to "Paramahansa." Without announcement or explanation, an extraneous "a" mysteriously appeared in Yogananda's title beginning with the July-August 1958 issue of *Self-Realization*. I have a copy of the 1958 seventh edition of *Whispers From Eternity* where the book cover is still imprinted "Paramhansa" but the title page and dust jacket have the new and improved spelling.

The change was unnecessary and raised uncomfortable questions. If Yogananda could not get his own guru-given title right, how could he be trusted on less verifiable matters such as union with God? If it was a minor thing, why did SRF bother at all? What had moved the mind that made that change? For there were ripple effects.

Yogananda had a distinctive flowing signature that was often displayed below his photo. This signature, of course, failed to include the new supernumerary "a." SRF's preservation of Yogananda's legacy thus came to include changing his signature as well as his name. SRF now corrected its guru's misnomer the old-fashioned way, using scissors and paste. If you look closely at the "Paramahansa" used by SRF since 1958, you can see how someone carefully cut out the first "a" from Yogananda, and inserted it after the letters "Param." Goodness. Why would something as insignificant as the spelling of an honorific title trigger such subterfuge? SRF's revision has appeared so widely and so long that most people mistake it for the real thing. Kriyananda, however, remembered how Yogananda did things.

Garcia took nine long months to rule on these motions, while we waited and waited. Finally, on June 21, 1993, Garcia gave us the good news. He not only affirmed, but expanded on, his ruling that Ananda could use the phrase "Self-Realization." Then he dissolved the preliminary injunction. By handing us this victory, he validated our approach to the case and effectively urged us on to greater effort.

Garcia Dissolves the Injunction / June 1993

Garcia started off the June 21st hearing by announcing that he would indeed, as requested by SRF, reconsider his written decision on "Self-realization." When I heard that he was granting SRF's request for reconsideration I doubted my ears. Looking over at Sheila's face confirmed my fears. We both started breathing again a few moments later when Garcia reconsidered, but then affirmed, his ruling in Ananda's favor—with a twist. He confirmed everything in his prior ruling except the part about SRF's use of "Self-Realization" to sell its goods and services. Garcia agreed with SRF's argument that the term "Self-Realization" was *not* generic when used to sell goods or services, and was instead "merely descriptive," informing the prospective buyer of the subject matter of those goods and the nature of those services.

Garcia rolled right on, however, to announce that SRF failed to show that "Self-realization" had acquired any secondary meaning. Ananda had shown that when people heard "Self-realization" they thought of union with God, not SRF as a source of "Self-realization" brand goods or services. SRF now had to come forward with something showing that the public actually identified "Self-realization" with SRF. This was what SRF had been claiming all along, and here was its opportunity to show that the public looked to *it*—not Ananda—as *the* place to purchase Self-realization-related goods and services.

But SRF's evidence showed no such thing. Garcia observed how its evidence only showed that SRF's members and suppliers thought of SRF when they heard the term "Self-Realization." It was neither surprising nor significant that SRF's members and suppliers thought about the organization when they heard part of its name. And SRF had no evidence that the general public connected "Self-realization" with SRF when

73

looking to buy Self-realization-related goods and services. There was no evidence the public knew who SRF was at all. The mark was indeed descriptive, but without secondary meaning.

Help sometimes comes neither looked for nor welcomed. We groused about SRF's reconsideration motion when we received it, but later found reason to be thankful. By granting SRF's request for reconsideration, acknowledging the "descriptive" nature of the mark, and then finding no secondary meaning, Garcia had insulated his decision against appeal. The appeals court judges would later agree with his approach and conclusion, and uphold both of his "Self-Realization" rulings as modified.

In more good news, Garcia granted Ananda's two service mark motions, agreeing that SRF did not use the name "Paramahansa Yogananda" like a service mark would be used. Because SRF used Yogananda's name only to describe its founder and guru, Ananda could use the name as well. And because SRF lacked legal protection for its uses of "Self-realization" and "Paramahansa Yogananda," no preliminary injunction was needed. Indeed, it no longer appeared likely that SRF would win the lawsuit, and Garcia seemed doubtful whether SRF really had the facts to support its many claims. Mellifluous news flowed down from Garcia's bench so fast it was hard to drink it all in. His Honor finished up by ordering Ananda to submit a proposed order canceling SRF's federal and state marks. Yes, sir.

The legal team walked out of the courthouse under clear blue skies. It was a bright June day, still early and cool, as we sauntered down the boulevard to celebrate at the Il Fornaio Restaurant with food and bubbling conversation. We were now in charge of a different case. Two years earlier the cause was almost lost, and now we seemed on track to victory. And as we pushed, we learned. Ananda had not been the first organization inspired by Yogananda that changed its name.

In late 1920 Yogananda set up his first U.S. organization, called simply "Sat-Sanga," in an office in Boston. With the move to Los Ange-

les in 1925, Yogananda changed its name to "Sat-Sanga and Yogoda," reflecting an increased emphasis on his "Yogoda" system of practical metaphysics. By 1928 the name had morphed into the more familiar "Yogoda and Sat-Sanga Society." The following year Yogananda formed a new National Yogoda Society, based in Marion Station, Pennsylvania, and changed the Los Angeles organization's name to "Yogoda and Sat-Sanga Society of America," distinguishing it from the similarly named Indian organization. During the dark days of 1930 the name blossomed into the affirmation-laden "Yogoda Sat-Sanga Art of Super-Living Society of America."

In 1933 Yogananda decided it was time for a change to something less exotic and more informative—something more suitable to the changing times. References to "Self-realization" began appearing in Yogananda's talks, letters, and articles in the early 1930s. The January 1933 East-West Magazine, *although still published by the Yogoda Sat-Sanga Society, was now described as the "official organ of the Self-Realization Fellowship of America." By the next spring the magazine was being published by the "Self-Realization Fellowship (Yogoda Sat-Sanga Society)." The Self-Realization Fellowship Church, Inc. incorporated the following year, and began using its now official name. After Yogananda's return from India in 1936, SRF dropped all references to Yogoda Sat-Sanga in the U.S., although the Indian organization continues to use the YSS name to this day. The mission mattered, not the name.*

Ananda once told Garcia that if he lifted the injunction, it would change its legal name to Ananda Church of Self-Realization, with "Ananda" formally part of the name. When Garcia dissolved the injunction he placed no limits on what name Ananda could use. Ananda was now free to change back to "Church of Self-Realization," the name that triggered the lawsuit. Nonetheless, Ananda followed through on its word. The confusion that SRF feared never happened. The world still turns.

Chapter 6

THE AUTOBIOGRAPHY

June–August 1992

Garcia's June 26, 1992 ruling expressly placed several key works in the public domain, including the 1949 *Whispers From Eternity, Cosmic Chants* (1938) and other lesser-known works such as *Attributes of Success* (1944). We were to discover that the decision, without mentioning the work by name, also negated SRF's claim to the copyright in the *Autobiography of a Yogi*, recognized as one of the hundred most significant spiritual works of the twentieth century.

Yogananda worked on his *Autobiography* for decades. Some trace its origins back to his 1916 trip to Japan, and he referred to it over the years under a variety of names, including *Yogi Saints of India*. Yogananda believed the *Autobiography* to be his crowning work, and he carefully took out the copyright in his own name. SRF had maintained printing facilities at Mt. Washington since the late 1920s, and by the war years was printing the magazine on site. In-house publication costs ran so high that Yogananda sometimes encouraged donations so they would not have to "fire the printer." But in-house publishing would not do for the *Autobiography*. Yogananda wanted the printing quality, and the distribution connections, of a major publisher. That meant a New York house.

In the spring of 1944, with the book taking final shape, Yogananda sent his trusted editor Laurie Pratt, later known as Tara Mata, back East to secure an appropriate publisher. She settled with her daughter in a house on Long Island, and after two years of effort produced results. An expatriate Romanian scholar named Dagobert D. Runes started the Philosophical Library in 1941, to publish the works of European intellectuals recently forced to flee their homelands. By 1946 the house had acquired a sufficient cachet that Yogananda predicted the book's publication would "bring millions to the work." On August 12, 1946, Pratt signed the Publishing Agreement as Yogananda's attorney-in-fact, and four months later the first shipment of books was on its way to Mt. Washington.

During the *Autobiography's* first ten years, eight English language editions appeared, three in England and five in the United States. Minor changes were made to the second printing, and the third edition of 1951 contained an update that we know came from Yogananda's own hand. On October 28, 1953, SRF purchased the publishing rights to the *Autobiography* from the Philosophical Library, an event reported in the *Self-Realization Magazine* that next month. For the next three annual "editions" of the *Autobiography* from 1954 to 1956, SRF made no substantial changes. In the eighth edition of 1957, however, SRF made hundreds of changes to the text that modified, often dramatically, what Yogananda had written. These changes included minimizing the role that Yogananda played vis-à-vis his organizations, and augmenting SRF's organizational power and authority. SRF dutifully renewed the copyright to the *Autobiography* in 1974.

Garcia's copyright ruling required more than one reading. Our motion addressed only those works that were originally copyrighted by Yogananda *and* then renewed by someone else after Yogananda's death. The order confirmed that certain books had been removed from the lawsuit, and placed on the world's bookshelf. This was a major step forward for two reasons: the lawsuit had just shrunk significantly concerning some key works, and we had confirmation that SRF was making claims it could not support with evidence. As one team member observed, "SRF's complaint was writing checks its facts couldn't cash."

Reading the order once again, I felt there was more here, something I had been told, or knew, but forgotten. I sometimes have that feeling standing in a grocery store aisle, with a vague memory of my wife's lips forming the name of a food item I was supposed to pick up. Maybe it was the smell of gardenia through the window, but I suddenly remembered that other book that Yogananda had copyrighted, and that SRF had renewed after 1952. Could we have won the *Autobiography* without even asking for it? Had SRF lost a crown jewel without realizing it was at risk? Or was that why the complaint had never mentioned it?

Turning to the files, I found both the original publishing agreement signed by Laurie Pratt in 1946, and the 1953 assignment of those rights to SRF. A quick read revealed that SRF did not buy the *copyright* to the *Autobiography* in 1953, and had purchased only those publishing rights that the Philosophical Library had received through its 1946 agreement with Yogananda. Yogananda held on to the copyright. When the initial term of the copyright expired in 1974, SRF lacked any legally recognized grounds to renew. Only Yogananda's heirs could renew the copyright, but they knew nothing about these things and filed no papers. SRF had filed paperwork that purported to renew the copyright, and perhaps even thought the copyright renewed. But because the Copyright Act did not authorize SRF to renew, those papers were a nullity and the copyright had lapsed—back in 1974. At that moment the 1946 publishing agreement became worthless, and its 1953 assignment to SRF more so. SRF not only lacked any copyright in Yogananda's masterpiece, but had lost that copyright eighteen years earlier. Did they know?

I remembered reading about SRF's 1953 announcement that it had acquired the *Autobiography,* and wondered whether that article might show SRF's thinking at the time. The magazine came out bi-monthly those days, and retrieving a copy of the November-December 1953 issue, I started flipping through the pages. Sure enough, there it was on page 34: "SRF Acquires Rights in 'Autobiography of a Yogi.'" The article claimed that SRF had been assigned "all right, title, and interest in *Autobiography of a Yogi* by Paramhansa Yogananda, including all rights in the American edition as well as editions published or to be published in foreign lands." The book "will henceforth be issued in America by Self-Realization Publishing House," with the next printing expected in December 1953. The article was wrong in every way. Philosophical Library gave SRF only *its* rights in the *Autobiography*, not *all* of the rights, and significantly not the copyright. From the beginning, therefore, SRF had misstated or misunderstood its rights in the *Autobiography*, and the Matas may never have known how tenuous was their claim to those rights.

When the legal team discussed this ripple from Garcia's June 1992 order, we realized Ananda could now publish its own copy of the original 1946 first edition of the *Autobiography*. In a single swoop Ananda would dethrone SRF as the sole source of their Master's teachings, and document the changes that SRF had made to its published works. Yogananda's centenary would be celebrated that next year and this would make a fitting tribute. But there was no time to waste. As forthright as it is quick to action, Ananda made its plans public, and told an SRF representative that it would be releasing a verbatim reprint of the 1946 first edition in August 1993. SRF did nothing. But the SRF leadership knew that Ananda's publication of the 1946 edition of the *Autobiography* would debunk all claims that SRF provided the world with Yogananda's "pure" teachings. They were worried.

The June order also got us thinking about Yogananda's heirs. If SRF did not own the copyrights, who did? Some had fallen into the public domain, but Yogananda's "common law" rights in his unpublished works might have passed to his heirs. It was worth pursuing, and the legal team put Vidura Smallen on the job. But for the moment other matters demanded our attention.

Yogananda began his mission by establishing residential schools in India. The year after Yukteswar initiated him a swami, Yogananda started his first school for boys at Ranchi, in the Bengal. Two years later, in 1917, Yogananda founded the Brahmacharya Vidyalaya school at Dahika, India, and formed his first organization. He named it Sat-Sanga, later translated as "Fellowship with Truth." Yogananda's guru had himself brought together religious leaders into an ecumenical organization called Sadhu Sabha, or "Society of Saints." Yogananda held the title of vice-president while in America, and became president on Yukteswar's passing in 1936. After 1952, the leadership of Sadhu Sabha, and control of its property, came to rest with a Swami Hariharananda. SRF filed a lawsuit against Hariharananda in 1987

concerning Yukteswar's old ashram, and the case spiraled into a Dickens-esque debacle.

Yogananda kept his first organization low-key. He did not want to appear to compete with his guru's association, and Yukteswar's own guru, Lahiri Mahasaya, had actually discouraged using organizations to transmit the teachings. Once in America, other matters demanded Yogananda's attention, but he never forgot his first organization. He remained in constant contact, changing its name to Yogoda Sat-Sanga, or "YSS," in the 1920s. When litigation forced the formation of Self-Realization Fellowship Church, Inc., Yogananda signed a will giving YSS half his property and made SRF promise to look out for the Indian organization that had started it all. When back in India in 1936 Yogananda executed another will to further protect YSS' interests. In his last years he feared, however, for the future of his Indian organization, and perhaps foresaw how YSS would become more a neglected stepchild than an honored older sibling.

SRF could not abide these adverse legal developments, and on May 21, 1993, filed a motion asking the judge to reconsider his copyright ruling too. Its lawyers scheduled the motion to be heard a few weeks later in June, so that they could circulate any order in time to recall all copies of the 1946 reissue before they reached the bookstores. Garcia must have been busy, or wanted to send a message, because he delayed the hearing date for four months, rolling it into October. This meant the hearing would be held two months after Ananda's August release of the *Autobiography*, too late to prevent its distribution.

Two days after learning that its hearing had been delayed, SRF claimed to have just discovered for the first time that Ananda planned to launch a verbatim reprint of the *Autobiography* at an event being held on August 23, 1993. On July 26, 1993, SRF rushed in to court with an emergency application to move up the October hearing date for its reconsideration motion from mid-October to "a date prior to August 23, 1993."

Ananda's opposition to SRF's application for an expedited date pointed out that Ananda had informed SRF representative Alvin Bass about Ananda's planned republication of the first edition during (yet more) failed settlement talks on February 5, 1993. Moreover, Ananda made its plans public again in March 1993, when it widely announced the book would be ready for the August centennial celebration at Ananda. Thus, SRF waited from February until late May before taking any action, creating a false sense of urgency. On August 2, 1993, Garcia denied SRF's emergency application. He noted that SRF had delayed in seeking reconsideration of his ruling, and then delayed after learning of Ananda's plans. With that double whammy he concluded this two-page order by noting:

> Plaintiff's application is, in reality, a motion for a temporary restraining order enjoining defendants from publishing and distributing the first edition of *Autobiography of a Yogi*. Viewed in that manner, plaintiff has failed to demonstrate either: 1) a likelihood of prevailing on the merits of its reconsideration motion and irreparable harm; or 2) the existence of serious questions and that the balance of harm tips in plaintiff's favor. Accordingly, the application is denied.

During the Ananda Centennial Celebration of Yogananda's birth, the 1946 first edition reprint was released as planned. It was, for the moment at least, available for all. It would remain so unless the Ninth Circuit reversed Garcia's copyright order. If the appellate court did reverse Garcia, however, Ananda might be on the hook for this additional claim of infringement, and substantial additional damages. Once again, Ananda showed it had the backbone to carry Yogananda's message to the world.

Chapter 7

SRF WANTS ANOTHER
BITE OF THE APPLE

July 1993

The dissolution of the preliminary injunction in June 1993 changed everything. It was a good end to a bad beginning. Most decisions in a lawsuit are not appealed, and only rarely does a single case have more than one appeal. SRF would file two appeals to the federal Ninth Circuit Court of Appeals, and then ask for a rehearing on one decision, seek a new hearing before a panel of judges from the Ninth Circuit, and finally petition the Supreme Court to become involved.

SRF filed its first appeal on July 7, 1993, to reverse Garcia's dissolution of the preliminary injunction. Normally you do not get to jump up and appeal every disappointing decision along the course of a lawsuit, and must wait until the end of the case to appeal. But a special rule governs injunctions. Both the granting of an injunction and its denial or dissolution can be immediately appealed. Ananda did not appeal Garcia's decision to issue the preliminary injunction in 1990, but SRF immediately appealed his decision to dissolve it in 1993. SRF hoped that the Ninth Circuit would rein in Garcia, and that the disasters of the 1992–93 campaign season could yet be reversed, before any real damage was done. Although we did not want to deal with an appeal in the middle of the other ongoing battles, and it ratcheted up the costs, SRF's appeal turned out to be heaven sent.

The law permits a party to immediately appeal the granting or denial of an injunction because injunctions present special issues. They are often given to maintain the status quo during a lawsuit, or to immediately stop some egregious behavior until the court can issue a final ruling. They involve a balancing of the plaintiff's need for the injunction with the harm it would cause the defendant, and recognize that the trial judge can make mistakes. This interim appeal is limited, however, to the issuance, denial, or dissolution of the injunction itself. It does not provide an opportunity to rehash everything that has happened in the case to date. But our case was not your typical case, and SRF asked the appellate court to reach several additional issues as part of the appeal. SRF's reasoning was that you could not decide the merits of the dissolution of the injunction unless you understood the key rulings on which the dissolution was based. Thus, the Ninth Circuit first needed to decide whether Garcia correctly ruled that "Self-realization" was generic, and "Paramahansa Yogananda" was not a service mark, before ruling on the dissolution. Even if the dissolution itself was not reversed, SRF might be able to glean language from an opinion that put the losses in some better light, giving it some hope along the long and costly road ahead. During this time very little of what was happening in court made its way to the SRF membership. But the truth would come out sooner or later, and SRF was already concerned about how the bad news could be packaged once it needed to be acknowledged.

The appeal provided a lighter moment as well. The Ninth Circuit had recently adopted a mediation and arbitration program for pending appeals, and we all agreed to give it a try. David E. Lombardi, Jr., an attorney who practiced civil litigation for twenty-five years in San Francisco, had been appointed to head the appeal court's civil mediation program the year before, and eagerly set up a session for us in San Francisco. Given the contentious nature of the dispute, Lombardi had immediately directed the parties to two separate rooms, so that he could travel back and forth in a form of "shuttle diplomacy." Because SRF was the plaintiff, he met with them first, while we waited for what seemed an hour. Finally, he walked into our room, not quite as confident as he had earlier appeared, and approaching Kriyananda asked "Are you Mr. Walters?" When Kriyananda confirmed his identity, Lombardi replied "You are not what I had been led to expect." Apparently the SRF representatives had been maligning Kriyananda with more than their usual gusto, and Lombardi had walked in expecting to confront some demon. After introductory pleasantries, and a discussion of the larger issues, Lombardi let us know that he was afraid this case would not settle today, if ever. The tone and content of his discussion with SRF led him quickly to conclude the obvious—SRF had no interest in compromise or settlement. After a rather relaxed if unproductive session, he thanked us for coming, and just before leaving the room he looked at us with an enigmatic, almost sad, expression and stated simply, "We must have compassion." We were all amazed that Lombardi had so quickly understood both the difficulties of resolving the lawsuit, and the approach needed to realize that resolution. SRF, however, had its reasons for appealing early and often.

SRF appeared to take every opportunity to play the money card and increase costs. And with no end in sight, Ananda began to feel the pinch. You cannot win motions or appeals if you cannot afford to pay the lawyers, do the research, and cover the myriad costs that Justice demands. Without the unflagging support of Ananda's members, friends, and community, SRF's "take no prisoners" strategy might have worked. The donors who gave beyond their comfort level deserve special laurels. Their support over the long haul, in good days and bad, through victories and defeats, lent Ananda the time and material to last the course.

Chapter 8

ANANDA KEEPS COMING

January–June 1994

Wave after wave followed upon the success of those first motions. From January through June 1994, we filed four successive motions carving away more of SRF's remaining case. It started well when, on January 4th, Garcia denied SRF's motion to reconsider his prior copyright orders, and denied its request to restore the preliminary injunction. Never giving up may not always be a virtue.

Three weeks later Ananda filed another summary adjudication motion addressing some of the few "Remaining Copyright Issues." Three days after that, on January 27, we followed up with a motion to invalidate the copyrights that SRF claimed in Yogananda's "posthumous works"— works where SRF registered the first copyright after March 7, 1952. This category of publications had been excluded from the first copyright motion, and it was time to start wrapping up loose ends. That February Garcia granted these motions as well. We rolled from win to win.

On April 22, 1994, Ananda filed its sixth summary adjudication motion, undercutting three more claims: (1) copyrights in nine older photos, (2) SRF's common law copyrights to things Yogananda wrote but never published, and (3) SRF's claim that it owned the "name, voice, signature, photograph, or likeness" of Yogananda. Grinding away, claim by claim.

As Ananda closed in, SRF had recently articulated another reason why it owned all of Yogananda's property. It *must* own Yogananda's works, including his common law copyrights, because Yogananda could not own them himself. As a *sannyasi*, Yogananda had taken a "solemn vow" of poverty, renouncing all property ownership, such that Yogananda could no longer legally own property. In addition, he had repeatedly confirmed, through his assignments and talks, that he had given away all of his property and currently owned "nothing." Because he had given all his stuff to SRF, the argument went, it now owned everything he would otherwise have owned himself, had he not taken that solemn vow. Ananda responded that Yogananda had taken only an "informal vow" of poverty, not some total renunciation of property like you might find among cloistered monks in a hilltop abbey. Moreover, SRF's own documents showed, and its own arguments claimed, that Yogananda did indeed own property after taking his vow of renunciation. SRF claimed that Yogananda gave SRF all of his property in the 1935 Assignment and through the two wills. But if Yogananda could not own property after taking his vows in 1915, then he could not have owned the property SRF claims he subsequently donated to it. SRF's arguments no longer seemed to need factual support or even internal consistency.

SRF had previously introduced the 1935 General Assignment, signed by Yogananda days before his return to India, and we now raised the two wills. These documents showed that Yogananda *thought* he owned and managed his own property, up until the time of his passing. SRF pointed to the many times that Yogananda said he owned nothing, and encouraged donors to give their money to SRF, as he had done. But Yogananda said many things. Perhaps he spoke metaphorically. Perhaps his comments were meant as spiritual affirmations. Perhaps, as a guru, he told different people what they each needed to hear, based on their progress along the path. Who knows? Undisputable evidence showed, however, that Yogananda thought he owned personal property, and that did not legally, technically, or actually, give all of those assets to SRF.

SRF also argued that Yogananda had given SRF all of his assets "by implication." There was no express transfer of all of Yogananda's property, nothing in writing that actually gave SRF what it claimed to have. SRF inferred a transfer of all of those common law copyrights because of Yogananda's statements about owning nothing and giving everything to SRF. But the clincher was that SRF possessed the original manuscripts of Yogananda's unpublished works. Yogananda's manuscripts, as well as original tape recordings and photograph negatives, were all safely ensconced in SRF's vault.

The question of copyright assignment now became one of law: was it legally possible for Yogananda to transfer his rights in unpublished works by mere implication? If an express assignment, a writing of some kind, was required, then Ananda would necessarily win on all of the common law copyrights. If, however, it was legally possible for Yogananda to give away his copyrights through his actions without a written document saying so, then SRF must be given a chance to convince a jury that Yogananda did just that.

The technical and draconian 1909 Copyright Act provided numerous opportunities for a copyright holder to lose its rights. If you failed to renew on time, you lost your rights. If the wrong person filed the application for renewal, you lost your rights. And assignments had to be in writing. We thought a similarly strict rule should apply to common law copyrights. Under the 1909 Act, a statutory copyright arose only when a work was first published. Prior to publication, there were no statutory protections. Instead, state law provided for a "common law copyright" that protected a work before it was published, and lasted for only as long as it remained unpublished. The initial common law copyright was owned by the author of the work. Like other personal property, a common law copyright could be sold or transferred to someone else. We thought common law rights might be somewhat more flexible than their statutory counterpart, but the law was far from clear. One District Court case in Arizona went our way and held that some form of written assignment was required. The judge's order made a lot of sense. Assignments should be in writing and state clearly what is being assigned. Only in this way could you avoid both an inadvertent transfer and confusion as to what was assigned.

SRF put much stock in Yogananda's March 1, 1935 General Assignment, made just before his trip to India and acknowledged before a notary on May 28. This preprinted form, completed by typewriter, stated in part:

> For value received, I do hereby sell, assign, transfer, and set over unto Self Realization Fellowship Church the within books, lessons, monthly praeceptum, furnitures, personal properties including shawls, blankets, portable temple of silence, my handwritings, typewriters, mimeograph machine, cooking utensil—and all machinery, icebox, files, victrola, radio, and/or any other personal property which I may own and which is not described or enumerated herein.

The assignment spoke in detail, but only about tangible personal property. It showed no intention to give away intangible rights, wrapped up with those shawls and blankets. It did not speak to any future property that Yogananda might acquire. Conspicuous by its absence was any reference to Yogananda's copyrights. We know, however, that Yogananda was familiar with copyrights in those years, and took out many in his own name. SRF now claimed that Yogananda used the sparse language of the Assignment to transfer to it all property rights of every kind, including Yogananda's "name, voice, signature, photograph, or likeness." Section 990 of the California Civil Code, which first identified these attributes as protectable rights, was not adopted until 1984. I doubt Yogananda had these future intangible rights in mind on the eve of his India trip. There was also a practical problem with SRF's position. If Yogananda gave his name to SRF in 1935, he would still need to use that name on a daily basis for the rest of his life. So, there must also have been some form of license by which Yogananda received back from SRF the right to use his own name. But, of course, it made no sense to talk about SRF "owning" Yogananda's name at all. It made even less sense that Yogananda would have given SRF rights in his name just weeks before heading to India.

About this time in 1994 SRF's legal papers became increasingly shrill and pedantic. They now routinely referred to Ananda's arguments as "inconceivable" and repeatedly told the court what it "must" do. More than once SRF may have lost a good point in its lather. SRF's papers also began referring to "Sri Daya Mata," and "Sri Ananda Mata," but Ananda Mata's declarations were no longer worth the paper they were perjured on.

In April 1994, SRF tried to stop the slippage by further beefing up its "SRF owns everything" argument. SRF claimed to have just found yet more documents saying that Yogananda owned nothing and had given everything to SRF. Accordingly, SRF asked for judgment (1) on its claims to the "name, voice, signature, photograph, and likeness" of Yogananda and (2) that SRF owned nine specific photos. SRF's argument that it owned everything was now supported by an "array of new evidence" that "compels summary judgment for SRF." We were amazed that SRF kept coming up with more stuff, but it was always more of the same. Now they might point to some bylaw reference that thanked Yogananda for giving everything to SRF. Next they would excerpt some quote from a 1939 newspaper.

SRF timed its motion to be heard on Monday, May 20, 1994, when Ananda's own motion was to come before Garcia. None of SRF's "new" evidence added anything, or contradicted Yogananda's active management of assets in his own name. And these occasional comments did not refute the fact that when Laurie Pratt went to New York in 1944 to negotiate the publication of the *Autobiography*, she went empowered as Yogananda's attorney-in-fact. Yogananda knew what he was doing.

SRF's problem was that its facts rarely supported its case. A famous photograph from one motion, called simply "PY on Boat," illustrates that underlying problem well. This image shows Yogananda standing on a boat in full sail on the Ganges River in 1935 or 1936. His personal secretary, C. Richard Wright, is with him on the boat, and someone obviously took the photo while standing on the nearby shore. If the photographer's identify was ever known, by 1990 it had long been forgotten. All we now knew was that somehow Yogananda ended up with a copy of the photo. We do not know if Yogananda was given the negative or just a print, or whether the photographer meant for Yogananda to own the copyright. Upon his return from India in 1936, Yogananda gave SRF all of the personal property he said he had brought back with him, including a print of the photograph.

Over the years, SRF began to think that it owned more than just a photographic souvenir from India. When SRF sued Ananda in 1990 it claimed to own the copyright of the image captured in the "PY on Boat" photograph. Asked to explain exactly how it came to own the copyright, SRF blithely asserted under oath that an "SRF employee" had taken the photo using "SRF equipment." Pressed for proof, SRF finally admitted that it had no names, no witnesses, no equipment, no actual facts to support its sworn assumptions. Yogananda had not returned to India on SRF business. The two disciples who went with him acted as his personal assistants, not SRF employees. SRF, Inc. had been formed only weeks before Yogananda left for India and had nothing to do with the trip. The Indian homecoming was all about Yogananda and his first organization, Yogoda Sat-Sanga. So after all the fuss and bother, it turned out SRF owned only a fading print of an old photograph. The actual copyright was still held by that unknown photographer back in India, or more likely his heirs, who could have sued SRF for infringement. SRF's claims to the other photos all suffered from these factual infirmities.

On June 6, 1994, Garcia signed the order granting Ananda's motion on the nine photographs and denying SRF's motion for summary adjudication. The judge himself seemed eager for an ending. These six months saw SRF's case implode, and by the time we filed our last motion on February 28, 1997, everyone felt the end approaching. In May 1997 Garcia granted part of another Ananda motion, and then on his own initiative, ruled that SRF did not own Yogananda's name, voice, signature, photograph, or likeness. Judgment waited just weeks away.

Things People Say / 1992–1997

As Ananda's copyright arguments cut deeper, SRF turned to new and more desperate arguments. SRF now asserted that Yogananda had never owned any copyrights in his books because he had written each and every one of them as a "work for hire." But for Yogananda's writings to be considered works "for hire," SRF must have hired Yogananda to write those books. To support its argument SRF now produced a notarized

The author Jon Parsons from the earlier days of the litigation, when he wore a younger man's hair.

The 2002 trial team: (left to right) Richard Jones, Robert Christopher, and Jon Parsons.

The "war room" at the Holiday Inn during the 2002 trial. Latika Parojinog works on the endless paperwork, while Rob Christopher prepares Jyotish and Devi Novak for upcoming testimony.

The core legal team: (left to right) Keshava Taylor, Latika Parojinog, and Naidhruva Rush.

Some of the many Ananda members who carried the struggle into SRF's backyard during the 2001 Convocation.

Jon and Naidhruva outside her Mountain View apartment, taking a break from writing briefs.

Keshava, Latika, and Naidhruva, planning the day's next steps.

Naidhruva, Keshava, and Rambhakta Beinhorn, with some of the binders submitted with the first summary adjudication motion just filed in Sacramento.

"Voluntary Release" signed by Yogananda on October 20, 1939. In this single page agreement Yogananda renounced and released "any and all claims, if any exist or arise, for my services," in exchange for one dollar a year. Yogananda's continued employment was stated to be at will, and he agreed he would never "claim as my own any property or premises of said church." SRF claimed this document showed Yogananda wrote everything as SRF's employee, what he wrote was a "work for hire," and that he had agreed to make no claim against SRF concerning his writings.

The document showed no such thing. It only provided that SRF was not required to pay Yogananda a salary, and that Yogananda would not claim what did not belong to him. SRF could still pay Yogananda a salary if it wanted to, and it did. Yogananda could work outside of SRF, and he did. Yogananda agreed to honor the corporation's rights in its property, but he did not give away any of his writings or other creative rights. In fact, it was hard to make much sense out of this October 1939 Voluntary Release.

Nirad Chowdhury received a certificate in Sanskrit from the University of Calcutta, and after wandering as a mendicant, came to the United States in 1919 to study at Harvard and then Berkeley. He met Yogananda in Boston, ran into him again in San Francisco, and soon joined his Yogoda Sat-Sanga organization. Yogananda renamed him Brahmacharee Nerode and placed him in charge of the Detroit Yogoda Center, which he ran for years. Nerode published several of his own original works through the Detroit Center, and was the initial teacher for such SRF luminaries as J. Oliver Black and Florina Darling, later known as Durga Mata.

When Dhirananda exited in 1929 Yogananda dispatched Nerode, then in New York, to run the Mt. Washington headquarters. For the next seven years Nerode, now Sri Nerode, was one of the key "Hindu teachers" associated with Yogananda. On the road after 1932, Nerode lectured and toured back East, traveling with his wife Agnes and their young son Anil in Yogananda's old "housecar." They ranged from Minnesota to Florida, Texas to New York, setting up study groups, gathering subscriptions to the correspondence course, and urging people to visit Mt. Washington. He returned to California for the first time in years to speak at Yogananda's January 1937 homecoming celebration. That March, East West Magazine *reported that "Sri Nerode alone, during the past few years, has initiated at least ten thousand into the technique of Self-Realization. He has done admirable work."*

But Yogananda had left for India in 1935 without informing Nerode, who learned about the departure from Gyanamata, the former Mrs. Edith Bissett and SRF's second nun, left in charge of Mt. Washington during Yogananda's absence. And Nerode's relationship with Yogananda deteriorated after the boss returned from India a Paramhansa. Slights festered into recriminations, and in July 1939 Yogananda cut Nerode's salary in half. Two months later Yogananda fired him in an unsigned letter on SRF letterhead. Within days Nerode served Yogananda with a written demand for half of the profits from their "Yogoda partnership." Yogananda wrote back that there was no money to share. Nerode had to understand that they were all in the same boat. Yogananda had nine mouths to feed and "hordes of guests." Three weeks later, on October 23, 1939, Nerode filed suit asking for five hundred thousand pre-war dollars as damages.

Nerode claimed that on Christmas Eve in 1934, Yogananda entered into an agreement with him to split the profits from the spiritual business. Yogananda's first campaign manager, Capt. Rashid, had made a similar claim back in 1925. That case quickly settled. This case was another matter. Nerode alleged that their partnership should be dissolved because Yogananda had starting thinking he was God. Worse yet, "young girls are placed on the third floor near the room of Swami Yogananda and the older women are placed on another and different floor; . . . girls have free access to the rooms of said Swami Yogananda, . . . [and] the places of meditation maintained by the defendants are too secretive and ornate of construction." When told of the allegations Yogananda called Nerode a "chiseler" and vowed a spirited defense.

Yogananda immediately hired hot-shot lawyer A. Brigham Rose, who aggressively attacked the pleadings. Through a series of motions Rose eliminated the irrelevant and scurrilous accusations, but only after they had been fully reported in the press. When Yogananda finally answered the Third Amended Complaint in March, his lawyer dropped a bomb on the case. Nerode had signed not one, but two releases before a notary public on May 3, 1929, prior to leaving New York for Mt. Washington. In doing so he had given up the very rights he was now suing to enforce. These releases incidentally provide a snapshot of the Yogoda Sat-Sanga Society of America in the wake of Dhiranandá's departure.

One release referred to Nerode as the "acknowledged leader of the Yogoda Sat-Sanga Society in Mount Washington." The Mt. Washington "local Center" was self-supporting, but always subject to the approval of Yogananda, who headed the "National Centre" of the "National Yogoda Sat-Sanga Society." Nerode would work without compensation for the "Yogoda Sat-Sanga Society of America," which was "primarily a beneficial organization for the help of humanity along the lines of right living and right thinking." Nerode would never lay claim to "any part of the proceeds derived from Swami Yogananda's Correspondence Course, or his books, magazine, or any income of his whatsoever." Nerode could be let go at any time, and would receive for his services only "free minimum board and lodging." The releases covered all the bases.

Nerode still would not give up, Yogananda gave another deposition, and the case went to trial in December 1940. For six days the press wallowed in the proceedings. Famous supporters of Yogananda, such as opera diva Amelita Galli-Curci, were featured in front page photos. Rose grilled Nerode on the stand, but accounts have Nerode holding his own. Yogananda never testified. It all came to an end on December 10 when Judge Ingram Bull enforced the 1929 releases, entering judgment in favor of Yogananda on all claims.

Yogananda learned as he went. The bitter tuition of Dhiranandá's betrayal resulted in the Nerode releases of 1929, which would win that later case. And when Nerode threatened suit in October 1939, Yoga-

nanda had all of SRF's workers sign another round of releases, giving up any claim they might have to wages or assets of the church. As Yogananda explained, "We have to have business methods in religion but must not use religion for business."

A Corporate Body / 1992–1997

In addition to its arguments about Yogananda's vow of poverty and his "work for hire" compositions, SRF now boldly asserted that it owned the works in dispute because Yogananda had not actually written them at all! The works in dispute, it seems, had actually been written by a "corporate body," comprising nameless SRF minions whose collaborative efforts had been issued under Yogananda's name. The "corporate body" argument was very attractive from a legal standpoint because *if* the works had been made collectively by SRF's anonymous personnel, then SRF could renew those copyrights in its own name. Moreover the term "corporate body" is not defined in the 1909 Act, and few cases over the years have discussed the concept at all. This ambiguity might make it more difficult for Ananda to disprove the claim, and it was, therefore, less implausible than some of SRF's claims. What could be gleaned from the cases indicated that the "corporate body" argument applied only when some piece of work resulted from the blended efforts of many people, with no individual being identifiable as the author. And once again, the problem with the argument was the facts. Yogananda did his own writing and wrote his own talks. He authored his own works under his own name. He was far from a nondescript staff member, and his creative personality never merged anonymously into some greater corporate collective identity. The corporate body was another forlorn hope, another attempt at legal legerdemain. These off-the-mark arguments may have come from the lawyers, but SRF leadership played along, saying whatever was needed, even when those sworn statements negated Yogananda's role as guru in his mission. I could not understand the ladies at the top. Were they really hiding evidence and lying under oath, or was God acting in some very mysterious way?

Yogananda opened his Salt Lake City campaign on October 3, 1931. In the audience that night sat the Wright family: Mother Rachel, older brother Dick, sisters Faye and Virginia, and younger brother Dale. Dick, better known as C. Richard Wright, would later recall how Yogananda filled the auditorium with "tremendous force; his presence was unbelievably electrifying." The family met the Master after he talked, attended every lecture in the series, and took every class they could.

The connection must have been "electrifying." Six weeks after that first meeting, Faye, age 17, left home for Depression-era Los Angeles, to live atop a hill in an old hotel. Faye, later known as Daya Mata, would later explain how Yogananda cured her of a blood disease that earlier had caused her to drop out of high school. She would dedicate her remaining life to Yogananda.

Most of the family quickly followed, with Dick joining them on Mt. Washington the next year. Dick was a dynamo during those early years. He acted as Yogananda's personal secretary and provided yeoman editorial service on the first set of Praecepta in 1934. Yogananda placed him in charge of personnel and office work at Mt. Washington, and when Yogananda incorporated SRF in 1935, he appointed Dick to the first board of directors, and the position of corporate secretary. Later that same year Yogananda left for his sixteen-month triumphal return to India, taking Dick with him as his personal secretary. In 1937 Dick became the treasurer of SRF, and served as both secretary and treasurer for the next four years. But Dick fell in love. In January 1941 he married, left the board, and went to work for a living wage at the Lockheed Corporation.

Dick kept a detailed travel journal of the trip to India, filled with the anecdotes he heard and observations he made along the way. We have some sense of the richness of this journal from the extensive quotes that Yogananda included in his Autobiography. *The journal itself has disappeared.*

Mother Rachel played the matron at Mt. Washington, and received the name Shyama Mata. Faye became Sister Daya, then Daya Mata, and Virginia became Ananda Mata. Together with other Mormon women, such as Laurie Pratt, they formed a cadre of hard-working and loyal devotees. They would run the office and the facilities, the machinery of the organization, through the 1930s and 1940s. They would become the fierce caretakers of Yogananda's legacy.

Signs and Omens / 1995

There were wonders along the way. I had read stories about miracles experienced by Yogananda's devotees. Brenda Rosser, daughter of Dr. Lewis, tells in *Treasures Against Time* how her father was driving one winter night with fellow disciples Laura Elliott and Alice Hasey (later Sister Yogmata). As they approached a narrow bridge too quickly, another car suddenly blocked their way. A crash seemed inevitable when it suddenly felt "as if a giant hand were being pressed down on the hood of the car. We slowed instantly to a stop, our car still safely on the road." Kriyananda recounts another incident in his book *The Path*, this time involving a disciple name Norman Paulsen. As he drove the Fellowship's truck down the hill one day the brakes went out. The truck was picking up speed, and Paulsen feared he was about to hurtle to his death, when the truck mysteriously slowed down, to the point that Paulsen could pull it to the curb and park it.

One day I had a little miracle of my own. Returning from a Friday morning status conference before Garcia in May 1995, I was headed back to the Bay Area on my regular route down the valley on I-5. South of Stockton the highway runs two lanes in each direction separated by a wide grassy ditch. As I approached to pass a big-rig carrying a load of telephone poles, it hit a bump that rattled the carefully stacked pile. The top pole began bouncing around, and as I was slowing passing alongside the truck, I saw the pole rolling my way. Hitting the brakes, my car nosed down in deceleration, the pole now sliding off right at me. As I slowed, the pole launched airborne, and landed on one end, straight up in the middle of my lane, as if it planted in the roadway, mere feet in front of me. A moment before the expected explosion of metal and glass, the pole was gone, and I drove through open space. The pole reappeared in my rear view mirror, bouncing end-over-end down the road behind me and off into the ditch. The pole had landed perfectly on its end in front of me for a fraction of a second, and sprung back up in the air as I drove under it. Just lucky I guess.

Chapter 9

A HAPPY ENDING
TO THE FIRST APPEAL

July 1995

Luck had little to do with the progress we were finally making on the appeal. On April 4, 1995, the three appellate judges assigned to our case heard our oral arguments in the towering Federal Building in San Francisco. Appeals are decided by a three-judge panel, randomly assigned, who together review, discuss, and decide the matter. We had drawn three judges and were happy with them: Melvin Brunetti, David Thompson, and Michael Hawkins. Sheila and I had earlier divided up the issues for argument: she would explain how "Self-Realization" was generic, while I handled Yogananda's supposed service mark and why Garcia was right to dissolve the injunction. The appellate judges listened attentively, but asked few questions of either side. It was a good thing the legal team was there taking notes, for oral argument passed in a blur of fleeting impressions. We met afterwards and talked about the tea leaves, but there was nothing to do now but wait.

Three months later the written decision arrived. It was a published opinion, included in the official compendium of appellate cases known as the *Federal Reporter*, and the decision would thereafter be cited as *Self-Realization Fellowship Church v. Ananda Church of Self-Realization* (9th Cir. 1995) 59 F.3d 902—in the 59th volume of the 3rd series of the *Federal Reporter*, beginning at page 902. It was now usable as precedent in other cases, and became a little piece in the ever-growing mosaic of cases making up our "common law." The opinion itself was written by Judge Brunetti, and the other two concurred with what he wrote.

Brunetti began by defining "Self-realization" and introducing Yogananda:

> "Self-realization" is the ultimate goal of Hindu-Yoga teaching. The Hindu-Yoga spiritual tradition teaches that there exists an "Ultimate Reality." The Ultimate Reality is infinite, but it exists at the core of every person's being as the "Self." According to Yoga, the goal of life is to transcend one's finite limitations, like body, ego, and personality, to dissolve the barriers between the personal self and the infinite Self, to "realize" a union with the "Self." One prominent guru in this religious tradition was Paramahansa Yogananda, known to many Americans as the author of *Autobiography of a Yogi*.

In a not-so-subtle dig, he noted that "Modern-day disciples of this guru, this advocate of rising above worldly and ego-bound concerns, have founded two rival schools that are now engaged in a dispute about the intellectual property rights to such terms as Yogananda's name and 'Self-realization.'" Later in the opinion he wryly observed that "'Church of Self-Realization' sounded too much like 'Self-Realization Fellowship Church' for SRF to have peace of mind . . ." Was he suggesting that a little more peace of mind on the plaintiff's part might have avoided the problem?

As a matter of housekeeping, Brunetti first explained that they would accept SRF's invitation to review the related issues of the "Self-Realization" trade name and trademarks *and* the "Paramahansa Yogananda" service marks. The decision would decide more than whether the injunction was properly dissolved, it would reach back to Garcia's underlying decisions on the key issues leading up to the dissolution. The decision would either validate or undo all of Garcia's key rulings to date.

The judges could have dodged these related issues, but decided that "their legality is inextricably bound up with the legality of the dissolution of the injunction." They would not review Garcia's April 1992 order finding that "Self-Realization" was generic, but included for review his later, June 1993, order reconsidering his earlier order, and affirming it as modified. It was a significant distinction, because this later order had expanded the basis for his service mark rulings. In addition, Brunetti indicated the judges would also consider "the district court's July 8 order that the registrations of [SRF's] federal and state trademarks be cancelled." It was the first time the Ninth Circuit had ever been asked to review an order cancelling registration in the middle of a pending case. This case had apparently piqued the judges' attention, and they were willing to use the opportunity to make some new law.

Their opinion upheld all of Garcia's rulings that mattered to us, including that: (1) the "Paramahansa Yogananda" federal mark is invalid; (2) the "Self-realization" component of SRF's trade name is generic and invalid; and (3) the "Self-realization" component of SRF's service mark was "descriptive and without secondary meaning" and thus invalid. The opinion further upheld the dissolution of the preliminary injunction concerning Ananda's use of "Self-Realization" and "Paramhansa Yogananda," and it confirmed Garcia's order cancelling the "Paramahansa Yogananda" federal service mark. By upholding Garcia's finding that SRF had not shown "secondary meaning," the appellate judges officially confirmed that SRF was not as famous as it fancied itself. This decision also upheld Ananda's long-fought right to use "Self-realization" in its name, and to use Yogananda's name to identify its teachings. Having convinced the judges to decide these additional issues, SRF was now bound by their decision.

SRF received a consolation prize for its effort. The opinion reversed Garcia's determination that the "composite mark" of "Self-Realization Fellowship" was *also* unprotected. Ananda never asked Garcia to invalidate any of SRF's rights in its full name and had only requested rulings concerning the use of "Self-realization." Garcia had ruled on his own that "Self-Realization Fellowship" was *also* merely descriptive without secondary meaning. The appellate court's opinion found that in deciding the legality of the larger composite mark, Garcia had exceeded his purview, and they reversed his July 1993 order canceling the federal registrations of the "Self-Realization Fellowship" and "Self-Realization Fellowship Church" composite marks. The "composite marks" issue never resurfaced in the case. Thus, the good news for SRF was that it could still use its own name.

The decision also called SRF to task on its "Warning" against false teachers. For years SRF ran a conspicuous "Warning" in its newsletters, magazines, and other publications, alerting its readers that some people claiming to teach Yogananda's word were not using the "true" teachings. This notice irritated many at Ananda because it so clearly targeted Kriyananda. The appellate opinion turned this Warning against SRF, pointing out that the oft-published statement refuted SRF's position in the lawsuit:

> Most important, SRF labels many of its products with a warning that many other groups promote material with Yogananda's name on it. According to the label, these groups do not promote Yogananda's "true" teachings, and the only way to guarantee access to Yogananda's true teachings is to buy material with the Self-Realization Fellowship Church sign on it. In other words, SRF represents (in the warning) that "Self-Realization Fellowship Church" distinctively identifies its products and creates a direct association between it and its products, and a buyer who buys a product merely associating itself with "Paramahansa Yogananda" could lead the buyer to buy a product that is neither authentic nor made by SRF.

SRF's proclamations of purity had backfired, and ended up showing only that SRF did not use Yogananda's name as a trademark. SRF should never have said it did.

Chapter 10
ANANDA WINS
THE SRF LAWSUIT
October 1997

After that first summary adjudication motion Ananda rolled from victory to victory in Sacramento. By June 1997 the Ninth Circuit had confirmed Garcia's principal orders, and further rulings in the District Court had ground the case down to a handful of claims about some audiotapes and a few photographs. When Judge Garcia set the date the trial would start, he also scheduled a pre-trial conference for September 2, 1997. In federal court this pre-trial conference is a very big deal. You must have the entire case laid out with witness summaries, exhibit lists, motions about evidence, and your arguments concerning liability and damages, such that most of the trial's paperwork is done before the conference begins. The judge then makes decisions at the pre-trial conference that set the remaining course of the trial.

By that fall, it had become apparent to all that the remaining issues did not warrant the effort and expense of trial. SRF was already talking about appealing the copyright rulings. Garcia thought his recent ruling might result in settlement without trial, and ordered us to explore settlement with our magistrate judge. When the parties could not arrange to meet with Nowinski before the end of August, Garcia decided there was not enough time to both mediate and prepare for the pre-trial conference, and he accordingly vacated all the trial and pre-trial dates. We were thus freed from the distraction and expense of preparing for trial while trying to settle the case. But we no longer had a scheduled trial date to bring closure to the proceedings.

Settlement did not happen, just as it had not happened so often before. Representatives from both SRF and Ananda met in Pasadena, without the lawyers present, and discussed the issues and possible resolutions. SRF would not deviate from its position, despite the rulings against it. The board knew what it wanted, and was willing to gamble to get it.

At the status conference that followed on October 16, 1997, SRF voluntarily dismissed the rest of its case, so that it could immediately appeal the copyright issues. It was risky. If the Ninth Circuit reversed Garcia and remanded the case for trial, SRF could raise the dismissed claims along with whatever else was sent back to Garcia. But if the Court of Appeals affirmed all of Garcia's rulings, and the Supreme Court refused to become involved, the case was over for good. Four days later Judge Garcia signed his Order Clarifying Prior Order and Dismissing Remaining Claims with Judgment. The clerk entered judgment that same day, and when the clerk's office closed on October 20, 1997, the case was momentarily over. Ananda had won everything. But by now the original lawsuit had spawned a second suit, itself already heading to trial.

Chapter 11

THE SECOND FRONT

November 1994

Since November 1994 Ananda had been litigating a two-front war. That month Ananda was served with a new lawsuit, filed in state court, by a new plaintiff, with new counsel, raising new claims. Or so it first seemed.

Bertolucci's Tale / 1994

Anne-Marie Bertolucci was a vivacious young woman who became interested in Ananda in 1991, and after separating from her husband, lived for a while in the Mountain View community. She moved to Ananda Village in June 1992, where she became a "trainee" in the membership residency program. After brief stints at a number of Ananda-affiliated businesses in Grass Valley, by January 1993 Anne-Marie was working at Crystal Clarity, the publications branch of the church. By that April she had developed a relationship with her supervisor at Crystal Clarity, Danny Levin, a church minister and a longtime member. Danny, unfortunately, was already married, with a young daughter recently diagnosed with developmental disabilities. Realizing the mistake he was making, Danny talked with Kriyananda about his struggle. Danny tried, perhaps half-heartedly, to break it off, but in July he precipitously proposed marriage and Anne-Marie accepted. By September, Kriyananda was counseling them both to step back from the relationship. Two months later, when they had been unable to break off their affair, Kriyananda asked Anne-Marie to move to another Ananda community of her choice. She left the Village in December, and within days was back in a one-bedroom apartment in Ananda's Mountain View community. She remained active in Ananda programs and shared meals in the community dining room for several months until August 1994, when she moved out to live in neighboring Palo Alto. She departed giving no hint of the lawsuit to come three months later.

Sheila faxed me the bad news. The San Mateo County Superior Court complaint named Ananda, Crystal Clarity, Danny, and Kriyananda as defendants. It alleged six separate causes of action: (1) Anne-Marie had been wrongly fired from her employment "because of her sex"; (2) she had been fired because she complained about sexual harassment; and (3) the firing had occurred "in violation of public policy." The complaint also claimed (4) fraud, alleging that Kriyananda had said he would act in Anne-Marie's best interests, but did not do so. Finally, it alleged that Anne-Marie was the victim of (5) intentional infliction of emotional distress, as well as (6) battery, because she did not knowingly consent to her physical relationship with Danny. Now Ananda had to deal with an employment lawsuit as well. And when a supervisor gets too close to the hired help, it's almost always a problem.

East-West Magazine *announced in May 1929 that a new Yogoda publishing headquarters would soon open in Merion Station, Pennsylvania, a few miles northwest of Philadelphia. "Swami Yogananda will now be able to give his personal attention to the Yogoda Correspondence Course and he expects to reside more or less continuously at Merion, where he plans to finish writing the Yogoda Bible and his universal prayer book,* Sacred Demands.*" After years on the road, Yogananda was settling down. He still had not been able to spend a Christmas at Mt. Washington. He would later share with Rajarshi how the hectic pace of campaigning wore him out, and how he looked forward to writing for a larger audience. The prayer book, which would be published later that year as* Whispers From Eternity, *was*

almost complete; and Yogoda centers flourished east and west, north and south. The correspondence course was proving a practical way of staying in touch with the flock, and it appeared Yogananda's peripatetic days were past.

The writing would be supported by dues and contributions from members of the new National Yogoda Society, which had recently set up a National Yogoda Fund at Merion Station. Yogananda was going IPO in the high-flying stock market. A May 22, 1929 open letter touted the Yogoda Publishing Company, a Pennsylvania corporation being formed to own all of Yogananda's works, and publish the Yogoda Correspondence Course under his personal control. Mt. Washington would remain the heart of West Coast operations, and the "first among equals" of the Yogoda Centers, but the movement was now nationwide and would be based back East. Yogoda members had an exclusive right to early participation in the stock offering, and the Philadelphia Center led the way with a $10,000 buy in.

On May 23, the day after the open letter, Yogananda set sail for Mexico, jettisoning all these projects and plans in his wake. He wrote to Dr. Lewis that day how he was leaving New York "with a heavy heart. . . . We all have to bear our crosses . . ." Dhirananda's defection had undone everything. Soon visitors no longer filled Mt. Washington, and the correspondence course withered. The magazine missed three issues in 1929. When Dr. Lewis returned to Boston after a few weeks that summer in Los Angeles, he faced down a contingent at home that called for regime change. That October the market crashed. Soon the magazine stopped altogether, and Yogananda bemoaned empty rooms and peeling paint at the old hotel. It seemed that even Yogananda had moments of doubt and uncertainty.

When Sheila first told me about the rumors of SRF's involvement in Bertolucci's case they were hard to believe. The state court employment case seemed like a completely new lawsuit, alleging the tired cliché of an office romance gone sour. But after talking with some witnesses, it began to appear that SRF was indeed involved, and was actively encouraging and funding the Bertolucci lawsuit as a second front.

We learned that before leaving Ananda, Anne-Marie had reached out to a sympathetic SRF member who dutifully informed Mother Center of her situation. This SRF member had also lived at Ananda before, and I was told he too had been asked to leave. Over the years he developed close ties with Mt. Washington, reporting back about Kriyananda and his doings. Witnesses now told how this SRF member had escorted Anne-Marie down to Mt. Washington, where she was welcomed with open arms, and given all the sympathy and advice she could handle. She reportedly lunched with Daya Mata herself, and was allowed to meditate in Yogananda's private room on the third floor, now reserved as a shrine. Two such privileges would be rare indeed, and the more surprising for a devotee so new to the path. She was then given referrals and encouragement, and seconded back to the Bay Area.

Team Bertolucci / 1993–1999

Bertolucci's first lawyer was a character. Aylesworth Crawford Greene III, known on the street as "Ford" Greene, was the son of a prominent San Francisco attorney. Years before, Greene's father had achieved a brief if brilliant notoriety when Herb Caen's "On the Town" column in the *San Francisco Chronicle* mentioned his gay affair with an HIV-positive lover, long before such things became vogue. These were big shoes to fill.

In the 1980s Greene's sister became involved with the Unification Church as a "Moonie." Ford went in to rescue her but got caught up in the movement himself. Once he managed to extricate himself, he rebounded into a born-again cult-buster, active in the deprogramming community. He was one of several attorneys for the plaintiff in the landmark case of *Wollersheim v. Church of Scientology*, and despite kidney surgery and a disabling bicycle accident that had him out of the office for months, he remained an attorney of record in the case. In July 1989 the California Supreme Court handed the plaintiff a victory when it permitted the former Scientologist to sue the Church of Scientology on several grounds, providing for a variety of damages including emotional distress. For the next several years suing "cults" became a cottage industry.

Not long after I filed Ananda's first papers in the Bertolucci case, a burly gentleman visited my office and introduced himself as Eugene Ingram. He was a private investigator who had learned that I was on the other side of a lawsuit involving Ford Greene, and his employer thought I should be told about Mr. Greene. His information consisted of an inch thick document pushed across my desk. Labeled a complaint to the Los Angeles District Attorney concerning supposed "criminal perjury," it read more like a hit piece intended to smear Greene's name. And nicely done. Ingram was disconcertingly thorough in researching public records and tracking down potential witnesses. He included copies of police reports, criminal and civil complaints, and even declarations from former clients about Greene smoking marijuana in front of them. Obviously Ingram continued to monitor Greene's every move, and took advantage of every opportunity to besmirch the man. I assumed at the time, and later confirmed, that Ingram's employer was the Church of Scientology.

Having already met Greene I needed no introduction. It was informative, however, that the Scientologists would spend so much money and energy hounding someone like that, publicizing his personal foibles. So that was the way the Scientologists played the game. I wondered whether my representation might take me into a shadow world of litigation where surveillance and character assassination were tools of the trade. Would I be followed and photographed, former clients contacted, and unsavory rumors circulated?

During the middle of an unrelated trial years later in 2005 my office was broken into at night. I dropped by the office early the next morning to pick up my laptop and witness examinations for court, but discovered the window broken, my laptop stolen, and that someone had used the key in my desk to open the file cabinet. There were six other offices equally accessible in the suite I shared, three of them with laptops. Most were undisturbed. A couple desks had some small items taken, but no other laptop was missing, and no other file cabinets appeared disturbed. It was the laptop that I had used three years earlier during the SRF trial in Sacramento. I had no idea who broke in, but couldn't help but wonder.

Chapter 12

THINGS TURN UGLY

1995–1997

Despite Greene's credentials he was not getting the job done, and more experienced muscle was needed. Kriyananda had to be humbled, brought down using any means available. SRF now developed a new approach to the litigation that portrayed Kriyananda as some self-indulgent Svengali, with Ananda his befuddled following. If SRF could silence his voice, his following would fall away, coincidentally creating new customers for SRF's Yogananda-branded Self-realization.

Fads influence everything, including the law. Sexual allegations against spiritual leaders became vogue in the early 1990s. Kriyananda had been around long enough, through the wild 1960s and 70s, that there had to be something out there. SRF already knew about Kriyananda's earlier "spiritual marriage," an actual marriage to Rosanna Golia in 1985, and Ananda's attempts at a monastic lifestyle. Local SRF contacts comforted those who left the community, staying in touch with any who remained unhappy. The situation now required SRF finding, and throwing, some dirt.

The Ladies / April 1995

The case took a troubling turn in April 1995, when declarations started appearing in the mailboxes of residents at the Village. The declarations looked like legal documents prepared for filing in the Bertolucci case, but they were unsigned, and the declarants' identities reduced to initials. The seven declarations all described some interaction the declarant had with Kriyananda during the previous thirty years. A few declarations seemed harmless, involving things like Kriyananda skinny-dipping in the late 1960s. Others, however, described in salacious detail a passing sexual relationship with Kriyananda that had occurred years before.

The declarations were written by lawyers, and we had learned from the McKean declaration that a declarant had to be questioned before her real story could be known. But these facts were so detailed, and the identities of some people so transparent, that I thought there must be some truth behind the ranting. Were these encounters between fellow pilgrims on the path, or had Kriyananda abused a position of spiritual leader, and forced himself on followers? It may or may not be relevant to the employment lawsuit, but it mattered to me. And, as intended, the allegations themselves sowed discord in those ranks upon which the community and the litigation depended. This tactic of creating dummy declarations attacking Kriyananda and distributing them surreptitiously, surpassed anything we had seen so far from Greene. It attempted to poison the well of both public opinion and Ananda's support base. Plaintiff's game had become subtly sinister, and that worried me as much as the declarations. I wondered more than once whether the declarations were true at all, or made up simply to shock and awe.

By this time I had worked closely with Kriyananda for several years, and had seen him in good times and bad. I had never seen a sign of impropriety. Positions in the church and at the Village were staffed with many women who I knew held their own opinions and did not hesitate to express them. I saw no sign at Ananda of any disrespect or impropriety toward women. Moreover, the people I met at the Village were vibrant, active types, not brainwashed automatons. I never saw Kriyananda telling people what to do, and had come to some understanding why people respected him. Erudite and disaffecting, he is always a witty conversationalist. A scholar and a gentleman, he lectures internationally and composes music, poetry, and plays. The declarations of these ladies did not reflect the man I knew, and their aging claims needed both clarification and proof. Whatever had happened, the Kriyananda I knew was not the villain portrayed in the declarations. But what had happened back then? And what was going on now?

And how had Greene found all these women, and then persuaded them to give statements? Most appeared to be already associated with SRF in some way, and maybe there would be merit badges awarded later. But why would an attendee at an Ananda retreat thirty years ago remember some passing incident, and now come forward to share it? How do you go about finding a woman like that after so many years? Someone had to be combing through SRF databases. And the ladies seemed eager to help, reaching deep for those details that can make all the difference in a story's telling. What was their motivation? Was this the venting of long-pent emotions, the chance to take center stage, or just more of SRF reinventing the past? Most of the ladies had no apparent reason to lie, and I assumed their story reflected some memory of what had happened back then. A couple of the ladies clearly had an agenda, and one was none other than Kimberly Moore, who long-time residents remembered as Kriyananda's former "spiritual wife."

As I read the troubling declarations more carefully, some concerned me less. Kimberly Moore, for example, had been introduced to a stunned Ananda Village in 1981 as "Parameshwari," Kriyananda's soul mate. They had met while he was vacationing in Hawaii and apparently shared an immediate attraction. For months she served as a kind of First Lady to the Village, and presided ceremoniously at many community events. They exchanged vows at a beach, and lived together at the Village, holding themselves out as having a committed relationship. They toured Europe together, and at the time some members were concerned whether Kriyananda would ever return to the Village. The relationship between Kriyananda and Parameshwari was apparently all very spiritual and elevated, but I doubt anyone at Ananda could have thought their relationship completely platonic.

Parameshwari's declaration now claimed that she had been raped as soon as she arrived at the Village. What? During her months there she had acted like a person happy in her role of spiritual mother. She left and returned to the Village at will. Had she really been raped, I thought, she would have complained, sought assistance, left the Village and not returned, or at least frowned more. At a minimum she would not have said the nice things about Kriyananda and the Ananda community that she did. This declaration, at an absolute minimum, looked seriously suspect.

Another declarant had been in a group that traveled with Kriyananda in 1969, the year he moved up to the land. Those days, to save money, they all shared accommodations while traveling, and this lady spent the night with Kriyananda in one of the bedrooms of a shared hotel suite. All was immediately known to the others in the group, of course, and upon their return the story spread through the community. When someone would ask Kriyananda whether it was true or not, he did not deny it. He did not equivocate or explain. He said he would not talk about that. Even when the incident was generally known and someone would press him for a word on the matter, he declined to talk about it. In those early days Kriyananda was not the guide and figurehead of an organized religious community that he is today. He was a co-owner of the land and catalyst of the community, which numbered maybe a hundred souls in the autumn of 1969. Many of the people in those early days were there for the lifestyle rather than the religion, and conjugality was not against the rules. There were monastics at Ananda, but the community included "householders" as well: typically married couples, some with children. I saw the evening's dalliance as no big deal.

Two declarations described massages that turned sexual, involving women who lived at Ananda in 1984. It appeared these incidents had happened, but not the way stated in the declarations. There was no compulsion, expressed or implied, and the ladies had teamed up to actively seek out Kriyananda's attention. Regardless of the reality of the relationship, it had ended in tears and thus must be Kriyananda's fault. The person who wrote these declarations for the ladies knew what he was doing, and I doubted it was Greene.

And maybe Kriyananda had stumbled along the way. Yogananda often commented that a saint was a sinner who did not give up. Whatever Kriyananda's position in the Ananda community in the early 1980s, if mistakes were made it was time to move on. These events from years before might tell of a pilgrim's progress, but they were receding history. The declarations seemed more a public relations issue than a legal one. And one that could be handled. The ladies would have to testify at trial, and through cross-examination we could place their testimony in the proper context and flesh out the omitted facts.

When I approached Kriyananda about the declarations he was open and forthcoming, until I came to the details about his physical contact with the women. He would not talk about it. Not even about Kimberly Moore, his declared soul mate, with whom he had a public and open relationship. What was going on here? Why would Kriyananda not talk about these events, even in a private confidential setting? When I pressed him, I discovered the larger issues in play. Yogananda had warned Kriyananda about the draw of sexual energy. If we are each given a cross to bear in life, this was Kriyananda's. He was to struggle in silence, and share this burden with no one. And he had failed. Twice he had shared his thoughts in breach of his guru's instructions. After Daya Mata became president in 1955, Kriyananda had confessed all to her. And he thought he had a confidential, almost confessional, relationship with a former SRF nun named Janice Moreno. Both had now turned on him, divulging those shared secrets. He feared to compound the error by discussing these things more, even if by doing so he might avoid legal liability.

I respected his decision, but it did not help the case. Without a clear statement from Kriyananda concerning what parts of the declarations were true and what parts false, and without additional facts to put these times and actions in context, the world would think the worst. Many urged Kriyananda to provide some simple, true statement to calm the waters. For months that felt like years, Kriyananda held his peace. At the time I kept thinking about that line from Isaiah, "He was afflicted, yet he opened not his mouth; he is brought as a lamb to the slaughter." I did not want anyone sacrificed on my watch.

When Kriyananda ultimately gave his deposition in the case, he explained exactly what had happened and why, under oath. He testified during his deposition because, given his legal duty to do so in the lawsuit, continued silence would place Ananda's future at risk. Once the facts were out, however, Kriyananda issued public statements and open letters that expanded on what had happened, and its significance. Over a hundred letters of support came in from women who had known Kriyananda for years. As the facts became clearer the hyperbole in the declarations became more apparent.

When we took the ladies' depositions, a fuller, more nuanced, story emerged. We obtained statements from people who had discussed these events with the declarants at the time they occurred, and who provided additional perspectives on the events. These incidents, whatever their moral timbre, were past history, and because the ladies' stories were all so very different from Bertolucci's, they were irrelevant. We thought, therefore, that we should be able to exclude both the declarations and the ladies' tales from trial. If they testified at all, we could cross-examine them, and put their stories in a clearer context.

Flynn Joins Team Bertolucci / September 1995

In September 1995, as Bertolucci's depositions were wrapping up and Kriyananda's about to begin, Bertolucci added some lawyers to her team. Michael J. Flynn of Flynn, Sheridan and Tabb in Boston had come on board, together with a varying cast of lawyers from the firm's Southern California branch office. I met Mr. Flynn when we introduced ourselves just before the start of Anne-Marie's last deposition. He pretended to know nothing about SRF, or whether this "Daya person" was a man or a woman. He talked about fighting the Scientologists on the East Coast, and the Rolls Royce-driving Bhagwan up in Oregon, and held himself out to be just another cult-buster. The way Flynn talked you would never have guessed he was SRF's attorney and a close advisor to Daya Mata. He denigrated monastic orders of the Hindu-Yoga tradition, complained about their strict obedience, and claimed they used chanting, meditation, and long hours of work to strip members of their individuality. With no visible sense of incongruity he criticized Ananda for the very practices that SRF performed every day.

I remember vividly that first encounter before the deposition. The deposition was being taken in a conference room and Bertolucci and Ford were out in the hallway, leaving Sheila, myself, and some legal team members alone at the far end of the room. Flynn came into the room at the other end, introduced himself, put his satchel on the end of the table by the door, and left, closing the door behind him. Thirty seconds later we were still standing at the far end of the table when the door burst open and Flynn lurched in without saying a word. His hand still on the doorknob, he looked at his bag, looked up at us, and darted back out closing the door behind him. Apparently he had left his satchel as bait, waited a bit for the hook to set, and then had sprung in, hoping to find us rooting through his bag. I had not seen a performance like it, and have not since. It should have told us more about the man than we took away at the time. Only later we learned that Flynn in fact knew who Daya Mata was, because he was her trusted advisor, and knew her well enough to call her "Ma." He wore an armband that Yogananda's followers call a "bangle," and appeared to be a card-carrying member of the SRF club. He began his involvement in the case by lying to us, and I doubt he ever stopped.

Flynn was not a member of the California State Bar, and to be attorney of record in the Bertolucci case he had to obtain the court's permission to appear "*pro hac vice.*" Among the requirements for *pro hac vice* status is that the applicant must be a member of the bar of another state, not a California resident, and not maintain an office in state. California residents must take and pass the California bar, and cannot use this case-by-case privilege to avoid becoming a dues-paying member of the bar. In his application to appear, Flynn swore under oath that he was a resident of Massachusetts and maintained his office at a specific Boston address.

The application seemed in order and we did not oppose it. Years later, however, we uncovered evidence showing that when he submitted this application Flynn was actually a resident of California, not Massachusetts, and was listed as the president of his homeowners' association in Southern California. He had a California driver's license and a California pilot's license. He maintained an office in Rancho Santa Fe and regularly appeared in California cases with high profile California clients. For example, Flynn was active in several California cases on behalf of former Beach Boy Mike Love, against the group's troubled founder Brian Wilson. He also represented New Age author Deepak Chopra in a number of cases. After battling Scientology for years, in 1982 Flynn filed suit in California on behalf of Ronald DeWolf, the estranged son of Scientology founder, L. Ron Hubbard. Hubbard ran his church's empire offshore, wherever his yacht anchored, and had not been seen by outsiders for years. DeWolf feared (or hoped) him deceased, and had filed suit to preserve the estate, estimated at $500,000,000, from plunder by the church, whose leaders Flynn publicly likened to "Nazis."

We found this out only after he had been permitted to appear in the Bertolucci case. After the Bertolucci case was over Flynn would apply to Judge Garcia to be permitted to represent SRF *pro hac vice* in the federal suit as well. But then we were ready with a complete record to put before the court. Flynn always seemed to be butting heads with judges whose rulings he didn't like. During one of the Chopra cases, Flynn took out an ad in the San Diego papers offering "REWARDS" of $100,000 for "information leading to the arrest and conviction of any judicial officers, and or lawyers, including retired judges and or referees who have received money, gifts, or other inducements" concerning the supposed wiretapping or burglary of Chopra, Flynn, or their firms. Flynn pushed the Chopra cases ruthlessly, and his firm made four judges so exasperated and flustered that they each had another judge take over handling the case. One of these judges was quoted complaining that, "In more than 30 years as a trial lawyer and Superior Court judge, I have never witnessed such misleading, manipulative, distorted, deceptive, vitriolic action by any lawyer or law firm." Flynn was making a name for himself.

Garcia had taken Flynn's declaration at face value and signed the requested order before we could respond. When we brought these additional facts to Garcia's attention he revoked his prior order and refused to let Flynn appear as an attorney in the case. He could still advise SRF, but he would not be recognized by the court as an "attorney of record." So Flynn remained active on Team Bertolucci, a grey eminence just behind the throne. This twilight world seemed to work for Flynn. Because he never joined the California State Bar, he could float from case to case untouched by the Bar's professional rules or its disciplinary system. As long as he got results, people like Chopra didn't appear to care about the legal niceties. No one blew the whistle.

But when we first met Flynn back in September 1995, we had no idea who we were dealing with. Kriyananda's first deposition in the Bertolucci case taught us something. Parties and their counsel have a right to attend every deposition. Several members of Ananda's litigation team would attend major depositions on behalf of the church, and it was common for ten or more bodies to assemble for a significant deposition. At Kriyananda's San Francisco deposition on September 11, 1995, plaintiff's group included someone Flynn introduced as Mr. Paul Friedman, a "paralegal in my office." Mr. Friedman sat through that day's entire deposition, dutifully taking notes. We thought little of it at the time. Later, looking into SRF's sale of some agricultural property called The Herb Farm, we discovered the company was being represented in San Diego federal court by none other than the Flynn firm. Flynn personally appeared in court on behalf of its owner, defendant Paul Friedman. We then learned that Paul Friedman was a major donor to SRF and claimed to be close to Daya Mata. He had facilitated the recent spin off of The Herb Farm property from its prior owner—SRF. In this way we learned that Mr. Friedman was not Flynn's paralegal, but rather his client in a federal criminal prosecution, and an SRF insider. We obtained the transcript of Flynn's appearance before U.S. District Court Judge Judith Keep in San Diego on October 27, 1995, the month after Kriyananda's deposition. During that hearing, when the judge chided Flynn for his overbearing manner, Flynn acknowledged showing "a little bit of intensity because in this particular case Mr. Friedman I know very well . . . and I'm familiar with [his] religious beliefs." So it seems Flynn gave Friedman a "back stage pass" to Kriyananda's deposition as a reward for being a client and loyal SRF supporter. Or perhaps it was so that Friedman could report back directly to "Ma" at Mother Center on how Kriyananda had handled himself. Flynn's shenanigans worked. It would not be the last time.

Daya Mata became the third president of SRF through a process of elimination. Rajarshi's short tenure and early demise left the presidential succession uncertain. Yogananda designated Rajarshi to succeed him as president, but had not laid out plans beyond that first transition. Rajarshi spent much of his presidency in either samadhi or a sick bed, with Sister Daya in charge of running the office. From transcribing Yogananda's lectures to handling his copyrights, and then running the business side of Mt. Washington, Sister Daya had gradually come to control the organizational side of the mission. Dr. Lewis, Yogananda's "first American kriyaban," had been ruled out of the running as the next president because he was married, and everyone now agreed that Yogananda had wanted future presidents to be unmarried. Sister Durga Ma was offered the presidency but turned it down. Sister Daya was the next best, albeit third, choice, and on March 7, 1955, more than two weeks after Rajarshi's passing, and on the third anniversary of her Master's mahasamadhi, she was elected president.

Unlike Rajarshi, who gave many inspiring talks before his presidency, Daya was not known for her grasp of the teachings. She never spoke on behalf of the organization and did not ride the lecture circuit, attending only a few Southern California talks in the early years as Yogananda's secretary. When the board sent out its March 7, 1955 letter announcing Daya's election, it incorrectly stated that she had joined the organization in 1930, although it was no secret she had met Yogananda in October 1931 in Salt Lake City. The letter further stated that in electing Sister Daya "the Board of Directors has followed the wish of Paramhansa Yoganandaji." The letter omitted to explain, however, that Yogananda's "wish" was that presidents after Rajarshi should not be married. To those in the know, the letter really explained why Dr. Lewis had not been elected president, rather than why Daya had been.

Yogananda's last letters to Rajarshi, written between November 8 and 27, 1951, and to be opened only after his death, displayed his concern. He lamented that "Poor Faye" was unable to take the pressure.

"Faye through my incapacity does not know to do things any way as I did, money or no money she has none to guide her as a result the work has started going back." He concluded that "Everyone in the work is terrified about the work's future." Yogananda once predicted that if he returned fifty years after passing, he would not recognize SRF. He was seldom more prophetic.

Kriyananda probably should not have sat for any of his depositions in late 2005. He had just undergone open heart surgery, and the doctors were advising delay. Had Kriyananda wanted to put things off he certainly could have. But events were now playing out at several levels. He did not want it to appear like he was avoiding testifying, and Flynn is the type of person who is best to get behind you. It was touch and go at times, but Kriyananda testified fully and truthfully, in the face of a bitter and sarcastic examination. And Kriyananda hung in there. We wanted to get his deposition done with, but as the litigation progressed, Kriyananda gave his deposition throughout, the last session in September 2002, a couple weeks before the final trial.

What's in a Name / September 1995–1997

Team Bertolucci liked playing games with words, especially kicking around the term "swami." They argued that the title by definition meant a celibate renunciate—one who had given up all possessions and desires. Because people around Kriyananda called him "Swami," the argument went, these people must think him celibate. And if they knew he was not celibate yet continued to call him "Swami," then they were deliberately trying to mislead others into believing him celibate. Bertolucci claimed that when Kriyananda let others call him Swami, he was validating the misnomer, and impliedly adopting their "representations" of celibacy. Under this perverse analysis, every utterance of "swami" by anyone at Ananda became part of a conspiracy to mislead the membership. It was nonsense, but nonetheless dangerous if the jury believed it.

Bertolucci's position ignored the actual definition of "swami" and overlooked the publicly known facts concerning Kriyananda and the Ananda community. The term "swami" indicates someone on the path of renunciation of all worldly and egoic desires or attachments. While sex may be a significant distraction, it is far from the only one, and perhaps not the most insidious. A "swami" seeks every day to reject the multifold temptations of this world, including his own ego, and realize his oneness with God. It is a journey, a quest that hopefully encourages and educates others, to be judged in terms of effort, direction, and progress. Bertolucci's lawyers did not explore the extent to which Kriyananda had advanced on the path, or what he had struggled with and overcome. They seized on one supposed aspect of the term "swami" and turned it into their litmus paper test. And they were wrong.

The term "swami" does not require or indicate celibacy. On this point we relied on Yogananda himself, who had explained in the Yogoda advertising pamphlets used from 1923 to 1933, that his own title of Swami meant simply "'Master,' or one who seeks understanding." Moreover, in Yogananda's line, Yogananda's guru, Swami Sri Yukteswar, was married, as was Sri Yukteswar's guru, Lahiri Mahasaya. We are told it was none other than the great avatar Babaji who gave Sri Yukteswar the title of "swami" while married, and Yogananda bestowed on a married Saint Lynn the "swami-like" renunciate title of Rajarshi Janakananda. There was simply no requirement that a "swami" be celibate.

And people at Ananda in the 1990s would not have thought Kriyananda celibate. Kriyananda had publicly renounced celibacy years earlier in the January/February 1982 issue of *Yoga Journal* when he announced his spiritual marriage to a woman named Parameshwari. In September 1985 Kriyananda had legally married a sweet and spiritual woman named Rosanna Golia. While people could put different constructions on his earlier relationship with Parameshwari, by 1985 Kriyananda had taken legally binding vows of matrimony and was a married man. During the nine years of their marriage, no one could legitimately claim they believed Kriyananda celibate. Kriyananda was still married when Anne-Marie became associated with Ananda, and his divorce in 1994 was discussed openly and often in the community.

It is hard to know whether Bertolucci's swami-means-celibate argument worked with the jury and tipped them toward their verdict. But it was all made up out of whole cloth, and only showed that Flynn, with the necessary approval of Daya Mata, would twist religious principles to wring some legal advantage.

The Bertolucci Worm Turns / September 1995–1997

When Flynn came on board, he immediately set about repackaging the lawsuit. The storyline became more dramatic: less lawsuit and more exposé. Bertolucci was now portrayed a confused waif who had been pursued, seduced, and abandoned by both Kriyananda and Ananda, who in the process somehow "tarnished" Yogananda's good name. I was not particularly impressed with Anne-Marie's heartbreak after seducing a married minister at the Village, especially with Danny's young child at home. Her pain may have been subjectively real and engulfing, but it did not appear to be Ananda's fault. And Kriyananda was just trying to help a minister save his marriage. The whole thing did not hold water, even with the histrionics about chanting and meditation, brainwashing, and implied celibacy.

Flynn took the case to a new, and lower, level. One afternoon a small single engine airplane flew over Ananda Village dropping leaflets. We later learned the pilot was Flynn's son, who had been hired to buzz the Village and litter the entire community with broadsides calling for the masses to arise and overthrow Kriyananda. What really upset the residents was the tactless and gratuitous statements made in the flyers, calculated to fall into children's hands. It was a stupid stunt, and as far as I could tell had no effect other than some passing upset and disgust. Perhaps that is all Flynn had wanted, a flyover poke in the eye. It may have violated the California Rules of Professional Conduct governing lawyers, but Flynn was not a member of the California Bar, and I doubt he had ever read the Rules.

Anne-Marie's complaint included an assertion that Kriyananda had behaved inappropriately toward her in some uncertain but sexual way. In May 1997, San Mateo Superior Court Judge Judith Kozloski threw out that sexual battery claim as well the first two employment claims. We were making headway, but the case was now demanding our full attention. In August 1997, therefore, Ananda and Kriyananda brought in additional counsel, Robert Christopher, a partner at Coudert Brothers, assisted by Richard Jones, to manage the federal case and its expected appeal. They would work with us on the federal case over the next five years.

In the months leading up to the Bertolucci trial the case looked challenging, but under control. Parts of the case had already been dismissed, and we thought we stood a good chance of excluding the ladies from testifying at trial. Maybe the case would play out at the jilted-lover level we thought appropriate, and in any event Anne-Marie's actual damages were insignificant. Flynn may or may not have been the embodiment of evil as some opined, but a greater force was steering the wheel of Kriyananda's destiny, and Ananda's with him.

Chapter 13

THE BERTOLUCCI CASE GOES FROM TRASH TO TRIAL

1995–1997

In late 1997, three weeks after entry of judgment in Ananda's favor in the federal case in Sacramento, the Bertolucci case was assigned to a trial judge in Redwood City. To understand how that trial would career off course, crash and burn, we must look back two years.

Trash / Sept 1995–Nov 1997

Michael Flynn awoke in the pre-dawn hours of September 29, 1995, to the clang of metal outside his Rancho Santa Fe office. Jumping out of bed and rushing outside, he caught someone red-handed taking out the trash. But this was not the private garbage service Flynn used. This freelance collector had apparently pushed open an unlatched gate, walked inside a fenced area, and was removing two bags from the trash bin as Flynn rushed upon the scene. With a screaming Flynn in hot pursuit, the man legged it down the alley, threw both bags in a van, and squealed off. But not before Flynn got a good look at his license plate. These events launched a fateful and unseen trajectory that would arc back towards Redwood City to land and explode on the eve of the Bertolucci trial.

Flynn quickly tracked the van through DMV records to a Peter Barranco and filed suit. When deposed, Barranco explained that he was just a student hired to do a one-time job by a San Diego private investigator named Jana Bolling. When Flynn deposed Bolling and asked her to identify who had hired her, she refused to answer, and pointing out that the Business & Professions Code prohibited a licensed investigator from divulging "any information acquired by her" as part of her investigation. She had acquired her client's name as part of her investigation, and she refused to say who that client was. When Flynn asked a judge to compel her testimony, the judge took the code to mean what it said, and refused to order Bolling to name her client.

Flynn immediately petitioned the appeals court in San Diego for an order directing the trial judge to instruct Bolling to tell Flynn who hired her. When they finally considered it, the justices bought Flynn's argument, gave the statute a much narrower reading, and concluded that a client's name was not the type of information that the Legislature meant by "any information." The appeal took time, however, and the decision granting the writ was not published until September 18, 1997, almost two years after the incident. Flynn had been busy in the meantime. He thought he knew who took the trash.

In the autumn of 1995, Flynn also represented Deepak Chopra in a lawsuit against some Chopra associates that had been filed by attorney Dennis Schoville, then with the respected San Diego-based law firm of Gray Cary Ware & Freidenrich. Schoville was a big name player in the San Diego legal community and had some headline-grabbing cases to his credit. Apparently Schoville occasionally used a private investigator named Richard Post. Without waiting for the results on his writ petition, Flynn filed suit on behalf of Chopra against Schoville, his law firm and Post, alleging that they were behind the trash incident. Schoville and Gray Cary denied knowing anything about the incident, but Flynn flailed away until the defendants brought a motion for summary judgment—requiring Flynn to finally show what proof he had. With no facts to back up his claims Flynn dismissed the suit.

It was still not over for Gray Cary. The firm put in a claim to its insurance company to recover the costs incurred in defending against Flynn's baseless lawsuit. When the Vigilant Insurance Company steadfastly denied the claim, Gray Cary sued. When it lost in the trial court Gray Cary appealed. The matter was not resolved until January 2004 when the appellate court justices in San Diego ruled against the law firm for the final time. The Bertolucci case tarred anyone who came too close.

In mid-September 1997 the San Diego justices in Flynn's writ petition told the trial court to order Bolling to disclose the name of her client. When her deposition resumed on October 14, 1997, she did just that. Her client was another investigator, Bill DiVita. Curiously, DiVita's office was not in San Diego, but in Redwood City, where the Bertolucci case was scheduled to go to trial that next month. Six days later DiVita sat for a deposition near his Redwood City office, and when asked, identified his client. It was Ananda, and Sheila his contact there.

The news about the private investigator and the trash incident hit like a bolt when Sheila told me in late 2007. No one had mentioned hiring a private investigator before. There were no reports from any investigator, and I could not remember any documents mysteriously showing up from some shadowy source. Sheila explained that as the rumors of SRF's involvement in the Bertolucci case proved true, she had suggested learning more about Flynn. Someone gave her the name of a licensed investigator in nearby Redwood City, Bill DiVita, and he seemed like a nice man when they talked on the phone. She asked him to gather whatever information he could about Flynn and possible contacts with SRF. During that call, DiVita suggested going through Flynn's garbage. Sheila told him to be careful and do nothing illegal. There was a lot of information already publicly available, and no reason to overreach. Too much was at stake. DiVita assured Sheila that private investigators went through dumpsters all the time, and the whole thing was kosher. They would wait until collection day and save the trash service the trouble of taking this load. A quick grab and go. I remember reading Supreme Court cases back in law school that allowed the police to use evidence recovered from bad guys' trash, teaching that you lose all property rights in things you throw away. Legal Maxim # 14: You cannot keep your cake and trash it too. I understood why DiVita and Sheila saw nothing illegal about looking through garbage that Flynn had thrown away. But this was lawyer trash, and it soon became grist for the karmic mill.

In late September 1995 Sheila received two bags of garbage shipped from Southern California to her Mountain View apartment. She opened the bags and started sifting through them. They contained mostly food scraps, junk mail, and packaging waste. Buried in coffee grounds Sheila found four documents concerning the lawsuit: a list of witnesses to be deposed, a draft of an unused declaration by an unhappy participant in some Ananda program, and two memos concerning Janice Moreno. Janice was a former SRF nun, who for many years had been a close friend and confidante of Kriyananda. Before hearing about their problematic pedigree, Sheila looked at the documents, decided they were useless, and put them away in an envelope in her desk.

She soon learned that mistakes may have happened during the acquisition of the documents. Flynn started beating the drums, making wild claims and tracking the trail of his trash. The receipt and review of the documents, followed by this troubling news, left Sheila holding a wolf by the ears. She did not want the documents, but could not let them go. There was no reason to return the trash to the Flynn firm. They had thrown it away in the first place and clearly did not need or want it. It seemed injudicious for Sheila to step forth with a spontaneous disclosure from which no good could arise. Besides, the whole thing might blow over. No harm, no foul.

On the other hand, Sheila could not now destroy the documents without risking personal liability for the destruction of potential evidence. And if she destroyed them, there would be no proof of their insignificance. Moreover, shredding the documents would make it look like she had something to hide. Yet holding on to the documents involved a risk that her actions would be seen as some kind of continuing violation. Back and forth she went between these two lose-lose propositions. The documents stayed in the drawer, where they laid for two years, out of sight and mind.

Trial / Nov 1997–March 1998

The San Mateo County courthouse has seen its share of big-name cases, including the Patty Hearst trial and more recently the Scott Peterson murder circus. Despite some poorer, more liberal, areas east of Highway 101, San Mateo County remains largely affluent, conservative, and parsimonious when it comes to awards. The judges tend to be no-nonsense pillars of the establishment, known for moving cases along quickly and efficiently. We should not have been in San Mateo County. Greene filed his complaint in Redwood City in San Mateo County, but should have filed it in the Superior Court for Santa Clara County based in San Jose. When served with the papers we had a right to transfer it to Santa Clara County. Maybe he did not know the local geography, or maybe it had something to do with Redwood City shaving an hour off his round trip. But we liked San Mateo's conservative pro-defendant credentials, and thought the venue fortuitous. Besides, Redwood City was closer to my office. We let the matter take its course.

When it became clear the case was going to trial, we enlisted the assistance of a trial lawyer familiar with the Redwood City court and judiciary. The legal team vetted and interviewed several small local firms, and decided on Gordon Rockhill of Redwood City's Rockhill, Schaiman and Carr, a veteran of countless trials in the courthouse across the street from his office. Gordon appeared to have the gravitas to lead the team through a trial of this stature: he reminds me still of Leo McKern's rumpled Rumpole of the Bailey, wise yet wary from years in the trenches. The team liked what it saw and Gordon was signed up before Kriyananda met him. Turned out there was no chemistry between them, and I know Kriyananda would have preferred someone else. But we prevailed on him, and Gordon was our man.

One of the many lessons this case taught me was the importance of the person-to-person relationship between counsel and client. A lawyer who likes his client projects a sense of rapport that often serves to validate the client as a person. The examination flows more smoothly, more naturally, and the jury picks up in subtle ways on the good vibrations. I doubt Kriyananda and Gordon liked each other, and it certainly looked that way. I know the trash incident hit Gordon hard right before he had to stand up and front the church to the jury. Whatever the reason, their relationship was another of the errant events brewing that perfect storm called the Bertolucci trial.

The case was assigned to Department 1, the Honorable Lawrence T. Stevens presiding. Stevens was a local boy who went to neighboring Menlo Park High School. He attended USC on a sports scholarship, ranking third nationally in the decathlon, and returned to the Bay Area to get his law degree from Hastings. He studied through the first Human Be-In at Golden Gate Park and the Summer of Love, receiving his degree in 1968. After years in Los Angeles, Sacramento, and Bend, Oregon, by 1982 Stevens was back in San Mateo County as an assistant district attorney. During the next four years he prosecuted murder cases, and led the high profile prosecution against a former police officer, Anthony Jack Sully, who was sentenced to death for six grisly, sado-masochistic murders linked to a cocaine and prostitution ring. The prosecution was news, and the Discovery Channel based an episode of its *The New Detectives* series on the case. That high profile prosecution raised Stevens' political stock, and played a role in his appointment by Governor Deukmejian to the Municipal Court in December 1986. Two and half years later Stevens became a Superior Court judge when the Municipal and Superior Courts merged.

We did not know it at the time, but when assigned our case Stevens was actively seeking appointment to the appellate court. A salacious case receiving lots of press could only help his application, and should a damsel be saved, so much the better. In August 1998, just months after finalizing judgment in the Bertolucci case, Stevens was elevated to the First District Court of Appeal.

Those days a case would be assigned to the trial judge on the day set for the trial to begin. The judge usually invites counsel into chambers to discuss the scope of the trial, and tell them about his ground rules. Stevens had received the case file that morning, and by the time we met he had only read the plaintiff's most recent complaint. He began the conference by announcing that the pleadings disturbed him. Of course, he explained, they were only allegations, only one side's story, but they were disturbing. Team Bertolucci had put the hook in him. Stevens immediately went on to explain that the allegations had not biased him in any way, he thought the subject matter interesting, and he would give both sides a fair hearing. Then Stevens gave us an opportunity to have a different judge, and requested that we agree for him to be our judge.

Well now. A surprising offer and a simple question. But San Mateo judges were known to push cases to trial, and it was rare for a judge to permit the parties to walk away at will once assigned to a trial courtroom. Rarer still for a judge to remind the parties of their statutory right to have him removed from the case. We had been assigned to him, and he did not need our permission to preside. We could object, but we hadn't. So why the talk about our right to remove him, and why ask for our express consent to proceed? Over the years I have decided that Stevens' comment and request were a "tell" signaling us that he reserved some doubts about his impartiality. He was projecting that we had reason for concern. I will not miss that again. When asked for our response, Gordon and I conferred for a moment with the limited confidentiality you get huddled in a judge's chambers. He thought Stevens was a straight shooter and we agreed we could do worse. Everyone was ready to go and further delay would be costly. We agreed he was our judge.

The trial did not start in September. Bertolucci had filed a motion for reconsideration of Judge Kozloski's order eliminating some of complaint's claims, and that motion would not be heard before October 14. Stevens saw no reason to rush, and Team Bertolucci hoped for a few more last-minute motions, so the judge set dates in October for clean-up motions and housekeeping matters. The news about Ananda's hand in the trash incident broke in mid-October, just as the final set of pre-trial motions were being prepared. Team Bertolucci quickly included another motion, this one for "terminating sanctions." "Terminating sanctions" refers to any of the numerous ways a judge can end a lawsuit without taking any evidence. This termination could include striking Ananda's filed answer, so that Bertolucci could then immediately obtain a default judgment, as if Ananda had never responded to the complaint. Sanctions could include instructing the jury that they were to rule in favor on one party on specific claims, limiting what Ananda could say or ask at trial, or simply telling the jury about what had happened.

Judge Stevens did not like the idea of one side going through the trash of the other side's lawyers. It did not pass his "smell test," and while it might not be technically illegal, Stevens thought it was not right. With the date approaching to select a jury, Stevens specially scheduled a quick hearing to take testimony on the trash incident. All the witnesses agreed that it was Ananda's investigator who had suggested looking at the trash, and that Sheila told him that everything had to be done legally and properly. Somewhere between those instructions and Sheila's receipt of the documents, something went wrong. Something larger than the sum of the people caught up in it. The trash incident should have been legal, undetected, and productive. It wasn't and it cost us the case.

For Stevens had found a means to his end. During the course of discovery, Team Bertolucci had served hundreds of requests for documents, depositions, and other discovery. Request No. 49 in the Fifth Request for Production of Documents asked for "All documents that mention, refer, or relate to" Janice Moreno. Ananda had not produced the two documents from the trash that mentioned her. I did not know Ananda had the documents, and perhaps it never crossed Sheila's mind that this request embraced the trash stowed away in some drawer. But Ananda had the documents in the drawer, and Ananda did not produce them. This omission may have been factually insignificant, but it gave Judge Stevens all the excuse he needed to impose significant sanctions. He decided to strike at the heart of Ananda's defense, and on the morning of "Bloody Monday," November 3, 1997, announced his decision.

When the hearing opened Judge Stevens appeared to seriously consider striking Ananda's answer entirely, and entering judgment against the church, and perhaps all the other defendants as well. But that would have been too easy, and Ananda might win that appeal, while avoiding the costs of trial. Something more spectacular, more devastating was called for.

Stevens concluded that Ananda had intentionally failed to produce two documents in discovery, that Ananda had benefited from that omission in some way, and that crippling sanctions against *all* the defendants were warranted on account of the two withheld documents. He ruled that as a penalty for Ananda failing to produce copies of the two memos from the trash, all the female witnesses—including, but not limited to, the women we already knew about—would be permitted to testify about all their interactions with Kriyananda at any time. The women could say anything they wanted to, relevant or not, about incidents recent or not. And there was more. We could not question, impeach, challenge, or explain whatever these ladies might say. We could not ask, imply, or introduce evidence indicating in any way that we thought their testimony was not true. And . . . the jury must never know about this order. The jury must think we silently agreed with the plaintiff's witnesses. During the trial Stevens once called me to task for grimacing at some testimony.

These witnesses were technically irrelevant to Bertolucci's employment case, but when we ignored them and failed to refute a thing they said, their stories acquired a growing visceral significance. Stevens' order that the jury never know about his instructions made it look like we did not dispute a single word these witnesses uttered. The order applied to Kriyananda's and Danny's defense as well. Kriyananda and Danny had withheld no documents and did nothing wrong. Yet they too would be the butt of Stevens' sanction.

What a blow. What an unbelievable blow. How could it be, that after so much effort and preparation, with so much at stake, we would have our hands and tongues tied at trial? With this single order the trial was doomed from its start. This was beyond reason or justice. It was cosmic, karmic, and darkly comic in a single mind-numbing coup. But was it some burning karmic recompense or just the gods having fun?

Juries are strange creatures. For days, weeks, or months they hear evidence from witnesses and look at documents, presented as a patchwork of facts. Only at the end of the evidence do they receive the jury instructions telling them what they should have been listening for. The lawyers then tell them what they heard, and what they should now think. Except in the simplest of cases, it is difficult for a group of naive laymen to grasp the factual nuances and the legal intricacies needed to reach rational and just conclusions that comport with the law.

Juries, like other people, make up their mind first based on how they "feel" about something. Once they decide who is in the right, they start selecting facts that support those emotional leanings. Juries act as the social and ethical consciousness of a community—but sometimes not to render justice so much as to resolve a morality play. In every trial there must be a good guy and a bad guy, and the jury wants the good guy to win. Much of trial presentation is communicating who wears the white hat and why. We were at a distinct disadvantage because Team Bertolucci would present its case first. They postured Anne-Marie as a starry-eyed ingénue in a sinister melodrama. Setting aside the actual facts, it was a good approach, and Steven's sanctions order was tailor made for their story. The case was no longer about Anne-Marie's employment or her treatment. It was now about whether Kriyananda had been celibate for the last thirty years.

Jury selection started on November 4, with opening statements the next Monday. Testimony began later that week with Anne-Marie. Team Bertolucci then started parading the ladies, and over the next two days four of them testified before we broke for Thanksgiving. During that five-day break the jurors had a lot of time to think about the ladies' testimony, how everything they said must be true because no one challenged them about it. No other story or interpretation had been presented, so what could they think? The trial resumed, another of the women testified, and then Parameshwari, now called Kimberly Moore, took the stand.

Whatever the ladies thought they remembered about these events, some now decades old, their stories came gushing forth. A few witnesses sounded scripted and others appeared overwhelmed now that their moment in the sun had finally arrived. It was all drama in high dudgeon, and we sat there and took it, day after day. Maybe it was cathartic, but it was not justice and it was not fun.

Team Bertolucci called Kriyananda as a witness, followed by a number of lesser witnesses. By December 5 it was time for the paid opinions. Their first expert testified over four days, followed by more "filler" testimony. Then Janice Moreno testified. She had nothing relevant or compelling to say, and her testimony did not hurt us. Ironically, the discarded memos about her did us far more damage than she did.

Bertolucci's experts were the icing on the cake. They gave the jurors the psychological justification they needed to find everything was Ananda's or Kriyananda's fault. The "power differential" inherent in the guru-disciple relationship supposedly stripped adherents of their free will. Although Kriyananda was not a "guru," he was a "swami" and that, it seems, was close enough for the experts. They testified how chanting and meditation and the fresh mountain air had all zapped Anne-Marie's brain, so everything that followed was Ananda's fault. Which meant it was Kriyananda's fault.

Experts originally developed the idea of brainwashing in the 1950s to explain how prisoners of war held in North Korea cracked under the strain of torture, sensory deprivation, and indoctrination. Modern day experts apply this same vocabulary and analysis to explain voluntary membership in religious organizations here at home. They call "coercive" any relationship where one person has greater "power" than the other. The trial became less about legal rights or actionable wrongs, and more about assigning blame for a lifetime of discipleship. It became a story about vulnerable maidens and manipulative cults. Beauty and the Beast.

Things could have been worse, I suppose. Team Bertolucci had threatened to call a string of new and so-far undisclosed victims. With Stevens' assistance, they could now do so, and say anything they wanted to, regardless of the reality. But the wave of new witnesses never materialized.

On December 16, Ananda began its defense, calling rebuttal experts and some of our principal witnesses. We got in a week of testimony, and then took an extended Christmas break until January 6. This timing also worked against us, because the jury now had weeks to think about the plaintiff's complete case, with only a fraction of the defendants' explanations in mind.

By the time Kriyananda testified, the jury was ready to not like him. They had heard days of negative testimony about him from emotional witnesses with nothing denied or explained. They had no reason to doubt anything the ladies said, or the construction that Bertolucci's experts placed on that uncontested testimony. And Kriyananda would not pretend to be someone other than who he was. For the last forty years Kriyananda had lived in a world of spiritual discourse and refined exposition, where he shared insights through subtlety and nuance. That approach does not work with a jury who has learned their law from television. Testimony must be scripted and rehearsed to be believable. There must be tears, some fireworks, and a denouement of retribution and moral resolution.

Kriyananda gave the jury his simple unvarnished story, as best he could with an order that made him watch every word, and prevented him from telling the whole truth. I imagine the jury found him stiff, too reserved, and overly precise with his slow measured delivery. This was the point where a better relationship between Kriyananda and Gordon might have translated into a more personable presentation, but It would not have made a difference in the outcome. Anne-Marie and the ladies had cried for the jury, pouring forth their tales. The jury correctly thought Kriyananda was holding back, not giving them the full story, but they never knew that Stevens had ordered that reticence.

Yogananda knew the sting of words and a scurrilous press. He finished up 1927 with a series of lectures throughout the snowy North, including several stops in Michigan. By January 14, 1928, he was finally in sunny Miami, beginning two weeks of lectures at the Scottish Rites Temple. These would be followed by Yogoda classes to be conducted through February at the Anglers' Club. Free lectures were scheduled at Central High School, and posters had been placed all around town. These plans were cut short, however, when Miami Police Chief H. Leslie Quigg abruptly ordered Yogananda out of town. The local press reported how "Swami Yogananda, East Indian love cult leader" had "his life threatened by a delegation of indignant citizens" who burst

into a class. Under the pretense of avoiding a disturbance, Quigg then ordered Yogananda to move along or face arrest. For a while Yogananda kept to his "hotel . . . determined to stay in Miami 'and fight it out'." But he wisely moved on to his next campaign. Two months after this incident Quigg was arrested for the murder of a couple black men while in police custody. The evidence was good enough for the grand jury and Quigg had to step down as police chief. But this was Roaring Twenties Florida, and Quigg walked free. By 1937 he was back as chief. Sometimes you need to take a licking and keep on moving.

Ananda Loses One / Jan–Feb 1998

Our case stumbled punch drunk on to judgment. Unable to present any real case, we knew we were going down but refused to give in. The jury did not like the evidence it heard, and on February 5, 1998, awarded damages on three grounds:

ONE: Ananda and Kriyananda were both liable for "constructive fraud." Constructive fraud is very different from "real" fraud and does not require any intent to mislead anyone. You can be guilty of constructive fraud by accident. It consists of "any breach of duty which, without actual fraudulent intent, gains an advantage to the person in fault, or any one claiming under the person in fault, by misleading another to the prejudice of the person misled, or to the prejudice of anyone claiming under the person misled." Perhaps the jury concluded that Bertolucci had tendered her affections in consideration of false pretenses.

TWO: Ananda and Danny were both liable for "intentional infliction of emotional distress." They had messed with Anne-Marie's mind and broken her heart. The jury also found that they had done so with "malice" and using "despicable conduct," as the Civil Code defined those terms.

THREE: Ananda was liable for "negligent supervision." The jury decided that the church was under some kind of a duty to supervise Kriyananda and had failed to do so. Moreover, it failed to do so with "malice and fraud." The verdict never indicated just what Kriyananda supposedly did, what the church should have known, or how it should have acted differently. It was all about the other women, who spoke with impunity knowing they could not be cross-examined. It was all about the past playing into the present. The jury, fanned perhaps by the plaintiff's "swami" shtick, had built the women's stories into a modern day auto-da-fé. The jury never found any sexual misconduct by Kriyananda, yet they awarded $595,000 in damages against both Ananda and Kriyananda, and only $30,000 against Danny. Go figure.

This award was bad enough, but the jury's findings also opened the door to possible punitive damages. The jury would reconvene later and decide whether to grant punitive damages "by way of example and to punish the defendant." If granted, these additional damages must be based on the defendants' net worth at the time of trial. The possibility of punitive damages thus permitted yet more discovery, now about Ananda's and Kriyananda's assets. So we began with yet more depositions on February 6, 1998. Bertolucci hired experts to go through Ananda's finances and report on everything they saw. Kriyananda's corpus of writings, poems, songs, and chants was itemized and appraised. The so-called "housing pool," through which residences were assigned and maintained, was scrutinized for hidden assets, as well as an opportunity to further roil the waters.

The jury reassembled in February to consider punitive damages. They had not lost their steam and awarded a nice round $1,000,000 in additional damages—an amount far in excess of any justifiable sum. This portion of the award was clearly wrong, and we thought we should be able to eliminate the punitive damages by a relatively simple post-trial motion. Ananda was being punished for the testimony of the women whom Ananda could not cross-examine, and whose testimony could not be denied or negated in any way. And the jury awarded damages never knowing about Stephens' order tying Ananda's hands.

We brought a motion to strike the punitive damages award, and Stevens concluded that he had to grant our motion. But Judge Stevens did not immediately discard the entire award. Instead, he ordered that Bertolucci had to accept a smaller award of $400,000 instead of the full million, and if she did not accept this lesser amount, then the punitive damages award would be negated in its entirety. Bertolucci did not accept the lesser amount, never requested any different amount, and the punitive damages award was stricken in its entirety. So there was no award of punitive damages. By this time Team Bertolucci had other fish to fry.

Ananda Does Not Appeal / 1998

Even without the punitive damages the judgment remained a terrible burden. The trash sanction had doomed the case. It was unrelated to any arguable wrongdoing, and prevented Ananda from cross-examining these inflammatory witnesses as their irrelevant stories were paraded past the jury. We all felt that an appeal would be successful. But what did success on appeal mean in this situation?

The lawsuit had generated inflammatory coverage in the press. Local papers depend on headlines to move papers, and this case generated several. They all played up the "swami" and sex aspects, with little regard for the facts. For example, at one point Kriyananda obtained Judge Stevens' approval to return to India on business. The papers, however, portrayed him a "sex swami" now "fleeing to India." The continuing negative press was itself a burden that we longed to move beyond.

By now Ananda was stretched too thin. It had loyal supporters and generous benefactors, but everyone was stunned by the way this cosmic drama had played out. How could Ananda pay for an appeal in this case, with the second SRF appeal still hanging fire? And after spending a hundred thousand dollars and a couple years, a glorious victory in the appeals court would only send the case back for retrial, where we would have to do it all over again. More months of trial. More uncertainty and cost. And now there were two new lawsuits. Ananda decided it could not afford to appeal, even though the trial had been a travesty. Instead, it would learn lessons and move on.

The Lawsuits Mount / 1998–2000

SRF's twin objectives of eradicating Ananda as a religious competitor and discrediting Kriyananda as a legitimate teacher, had not been achieved. Despite the judgment, more was needed. Bertolucci now changed back to her unmarried name of Murphy and she and Flynn each filed another round of lawsuits against Ananda and many of its members and supporters.

On February 17, 1998, Bertolucci, under her maiden name Anne-Marie Murphy, filed her second lawsuit; this time captioned *Murphy v. Walters.* The Murphy suit sought damages for the trash incident back in September 1995. She asked for damages against Ananda and its entire litigation team for a host of claims such as theft, invasion of privacy, and engaging in a conspiracy to steal the trash. It parleyed this simple incident, far away and removed from Ananda's control, into an additional lawsuit.

Getting a third bite out of the trash apple, Flynn filed his own lawsuit against Kriyananda, as if Kriyananda had reached into the trash himself. The Flynn suit was based on the same September 1995 garbage grab, but sought its own damages for trespass, theft, and interference with business relations. This seemed like an awful lot of karma for very little trash.

I think Murphy and Flynn filed their lawsuits about the trash because Stevens had made such a big deal out of it. The trash was just trash, and Stevens' order reflected more spleen than reason. Now Flynn and Murphy were claiming everything from business interruption to emotional distress based on the incident. We thought at the time that Stevens had been wrong on the law, and it turned out we were right. Confirmation came as cold comfort, however, years later, when the Sacramento-based appellate court denied Ananda's claim for insurance coverage.

When Ananda was required to defend itself on the new trash lawsuits, it requested its insurance company provide or pay for its legal defense. The company refused to pay any part of the defense costs, although coverage included damages to the "tangible personal property" of another. The insurance company contended that Ananda had committed no wrongdoing against Flynn's personal property, so there was no liability under the insurance policy. When the trial judge refused to order the insurance company to pay the defense costs, Ananda appealed. The Third District Court of Appeal in Sacramento ultimately upheld the trial judge, and in 2002 denied coverage. In doing so, the opinion concluded that

> Documents which have been placed in an outdoor trash barrel no longer retain their character as the personal property of the one who has discarded it. By placing them into the garbage, the owner renounces the key incidents of ownership – title, possession, and the right to control. . . . Since all of the documents at issue had been dumped in the trash, the [two lawsuits] did not raise the potential of a damage award based on interference with or deprivation of their personal property.

In denying coverage the justices concluded that Judge Stevens had been wrong in 1997 when he determined that a "conversion," or taking of personal property, had occurred. The justices thought it was just trash, even though the opinion acknowledged that "the cost of defending the Murphy and Flynn suits coupled with the financial burden of the Bertolucci suit drove Ananda to the point of insolvency, and forced it to declare bankruptcy." This opinion, *Ananda v. Massachusetts Bay Insurance Co.* (2002) 95 Cal. App. 4th 1273, was another of the many satellite decisions generated by the litigation.

While in the bankruptcy court, Ananda wrapped up the Bertolucci, Flynn, and Murphy suits for around $1.8 million. That is a lot of money. Even then, Team Bertolucci continued to try and eliminate Ananda and Kriyananda as a competitor of SRF. There was a sustained effort to use the judgment to levy on, and buy at auction, the copyrights in all of Kriyananda's works. These would have little commercial value on the open market without a committed publisher, and should have been of no interest to Murphy or Flynn. But SRF would love to own, and suppress, Kriyananda's library of writings, talks, and songs. In January 1999,

Flynn prepared a sixty-eight page report on supposed "potential internal revenue violations" by Ananda and threatened to give it to the IRS. The hefty report took a lot of time and money, with the sole apparent object of harassing Ananda, but it went nowhere. It went nowhere because, despite the cost and effort, despite turning over every stone, it found that Ananda had acted appropriately.

SRF tried mightily, but did not get the copyrights in Kriyananda's writings. In December 1999 Ananda emerged from bankruptcy and stepped into a new millennium.

Chapter 14

A LAST APPEAL

November 1997

As the Bertolucci matters wound down, the federal case started picking up steam again. The federal court's entry of judgment for Ananda in
October 1997 had invigorated us, and even during the appeal let us hope
it was almost over. But SRF could not let truth and justice stand un-
challenged, and on November 18, 1997, filed its second appeal. Months
earlier, when the Bertolucci case was still lumbering towards trial in
Redwood City, Ananda had retained lawyers from Coudert Brothers to
manage the federal case. Their first task was the appeal, and they tapped
experienced appellate counsel to handle all of its aspects. Briefs were filed
pro and con, and for two years we waited again for word from on high.

Urantia Falls out of the Blue / 1995–1997

During the 1990s copyright law was being applied to religious writings in new and exciting ways. One case we had been following closely
arose in Arizona, and concerned the copyright in a collection of apho-
risms authored by celestial beings. Around 1911 otherworldly beings began to speak to Chicago psychiatrist Dr. William S. Sadler, through a
patient of his under hypnosis. The good doctor took it all down and
shared these messages with other receptive souls. He and several adherents formed a series of associations that started putting questions to the
beings. They gathered and edited the responses, and inscribed them on
2,000 printing plates. Dr. Sadler and the others then organized the Uran-

tia Foundation as an Illinois charitable trust, which published the papers in 1955 as *The Urantia Book*. Dr. Sadler registered the copyright that year in his name, and the Foundation renewed it in 1983 as a "work for hire." In 1990, the year our suit began, Kristen Maaherra started distributing a study guide on disk that included the entire *Urantia Book*. The Foundation sued that next year alleging copyright infringement.

When the Foundation renewed the copyright in 1983 it did so claiming that the book was a "work for hire." While the work may have been a "composite work," composed by many people, and entitled to renewal on that ground, it clearly was *not* a "work for hire." The celestial beings were in no sense employees, contractors, or hirelings of Dr. Sadler, nor he of the Foundation. As in our case, the Foundation had no documents transferring copyright, and had misstated the basis for its copyright renewal.

We first took notice of the *Urantia* case when it helped us. But the tide turned on June 10, 1997, when the Ninth Circuit Court of Appeals issued its opinion in *Urantia Foundation v. Maaherra*. In a decision written by Judge Schroeder, the appeals court reversed the trial judge, and held that a common law trademark could be transferred without necessarily complying with any formal requirements. Indeed, the mere possession of the original documents could be used as evidence to show that the author intended the document-holder to own the copyright. This was a sea change in the law, cresting just in time for SRF's second appeal.

The Golden Lotus Temple crowned the cliff's edge at Encinitas, a hundred feet above the blue Pacific. Gleaming white against the sky and sea, the temple's flat roof supported three golden lotus blossoms towering above the entrance façade. The blue tile altar overlooked the ocean, with octagon windows rising another thirty feet above.

Rajarshi gave the Dream Hermitage and its seventeen acres to Yogananda as a homecoming present in December 1936. Yogananda immediately envisioned a Temple of All Religions overlooking the limitless sea. The project was "conceived and designed by Swami Yogananda, who minutely supervised all the building operations." SRF's East-West Magazine *touted it as "the most beautiful and unusual temple ever built by a Hindu in the Western world." On January 2, 1938, just thirteen months after first seeing the site, Yogananda dedicated the new Golden Lotus Temple.*

The Temple became the showplace for all major occasions, such as Brahmachari Jotin's initiation into the monastic order as Swami Premananda. C. Richard Wright wrote in December 1937 that "the entire structure is mirrored like a lovely dream in a large pool by the side of the Temple. Palms, olive and other stately trees and rare plants beautify the grounds. . . . Never have such large gold lotuses been used on any other temple. Their sparkling glint in the sun is visible for miles around." Pride, they say, goes before a fall.

The Dream Hermitage residents awoke early on the morning of July 22, 1942, to the sound of snapping timbers and breaking glass. Yogananda and the members living in the hermitage jumped out of bed and raced over to the cliff, still crumbling under the building's edifice, the altar tilting forward, the windows cracking then bursting one after another, raining towards the dark beach below. It slid slowly at first, and the staff was able to retrieve the precious statues and several other items. Yogananda initially wanted to conduct Sunday services at the temple four days later, but was persuaded the risk was too great, as the cliff continued to give way. Over the next weeks the temple slid in noisy jolts down the cliff, becoming one with the all-embracing sea below. In a letter written late in life, Yogananda told Rajarshi that he had undergone five "crucifixions" in America, the Golden Lotus Temple being the last.

Events did not always work out the way Yogananda first thought they would, but he did not give up. The Golden Lotus would be replaced the following year by a new temple in San Diego, thanks to Rajarshi's continuing generosity.

When the Ninth Circuit heard the second appeal, our panel included Judge Schroeder, the author of the *Urantia* decision. The vagaries of the law, and the luck of the draw, were undercutting our beautiful arguments. But trough or crest, we pressed forward.

A Superior Copyright Interest / 1998

The *Urantia* opinion concerned us. The Foundation had received an "informal assignment of common law copyrights" to the *Urantia Book*, in the same way SRF claimed it had received the copyrights to Yogananda's unpublished writings. The appellate court now said the Foundation could enforce that informal assignment. If the Foundation could enforce its informally assigned copyright, why not SRF? There were many similarities between the cases, and the decision opined that "mere possession of the printing plates . . . may have been sufficient to establish an assignment as against a third party . . . who does not claim any superior copyright interest." SRF's mere possession of Yogananda's original manuscripts, typescripts, and notes might be sufficient in itself to show that SRF held the copyright. Moreover, after *Urantia* we might not be able to survive a motion for summary adjudication, unless we had some kind of "superior copyright interest." To stay in the game, we needed our own legitimate claim to the works that was arguably "superior" to SRF's naked possession of original documents.

We were already on it. Five years earlier, soon after Garcia's first copyright ruling, Ananda had set out to obtain licenses from Yogananda's heirs. If it turned out that SRF did not own Yogananda's common law copyrights, and no will decreed otherwise, those rights would have passed to Yogananda's heirs. Yogananda was a monastic, had never married and had no children, meaning the property should have passed to his siblings, cousins, and the like back in India. If the common law rights were in his estate when he died, then many heirs may each own some small portion of them now. If the heirs would license their rights to Ananda, we would have legitimate claims to the works that might actually trump the happenstance of SRF's possession of manuscripts. There were a couple tricky questions about California's intestacy law back in 1952, some issues about the international implications of the assignments, and practical problems of making it happen, but we thought we were on to something.

Ananda assembled a comprehensive chart of each known living person who should have received a portion of Yogananda's intestate estate. Now it was merely a matter of contacting each one of them, and asking if they would be kind enough to license their possible rights in Yogananda's writings to Ananda. We decided to request that each heir grant Ananda a perpetual, royalty-free, non-exclusive license to quote from and otherwise use any common law writings. This license would not interfere with the heirs doing whatever else they wanted with their rights. They could license them to SRF too if they wanted.

We anticipated that most of these heirs knew nothing about the SRF case, and needed to be brought up to speed on the litigation. They needed to be told that they might have unknowingly inherited some fraction of Yogananda's rights in some English writings. We should not overstate the likelihood of their rights, nor minimize them in the event they later become valuable. Disclosures were prepared, licenses drafted, and Vidura put in charge. He and his wife, Durga, were well known to Yogananda's Indian relatives because they had led many of Ananda's annual pilgrimages to sites associated with Yogananda's life in India. Vidura started making phone calls, and several weeks later boarded a plane to India with a briefcase full of documents.

Ananda obtained written assignments from three of Yogananda's heirs. Not many, but enough for Ananda to stake some legitimate claim to use of Yogananda's writings. These forward-looking actions in 1992–93 provided Ananda with some measure of protection in 1997, when the *Urantia* decision came down. For at that point Ananda held a legitimate claim to a possibly "superior copyright interest," as the *Urantia* decision now required. Had the second appeal not revived SRF's common law assignment, Ananda may have clinched that superior interest, giving Ananda rights in all of Yogananda's unpublished works.

Good News Sends Us Back to Court / March 2000

February 2000 found us again in San Francisco's Federal Building. Our panel of appeal judges this time consisted of Mary M. Schroeder, together with John T. Noonan, and A. Wallace Tashima. Glenn Trost out of Coudert's Los Angeles office had written the brief and flown up to argue the case. The matter was submitted that same day, and a decision issued just five weeks later, on March 23, 2000. Like its sister opinion of five years before, it is published in the official reports and can now be found in every law library and on the web as *Self-Realization Fellowship Church v. Ananda Church of Self-Realization* (9th Cir. 2000) 206 F.3d 1322. Given the relative dearth of lawsuits and decisions on these issues, it also has become a "leading case" on copyright disputes between churches under the 1909 Act.

The opinion started by observing the appeal involved a "litigation war between two rival churches," and summarized its holdings in two succinct paragraphs:

> The most important [issues] are whether the works of a religious leader, living under a vow of poverty in the church he founded, can be considered "works for hire" or the works of a "corporate body" within the meaning of the 1909 Copyright Act and, in the alternative, whether SRF has adduced evidence from which a jury could conclude that a valid assignment of common law copyrights occurred.
>
> With regard to Yogananda's writings and spoken lectures, we hold that the works are not works for hire or the works of a corporate body, so that the common law copyrights did not vest in the church as a matter of law. We hold that there are triable issues with regard to the purported assignments and remand for further proceedings on those issues. We also hold that there is a triable issue regarding whether some of the photographs involved in this appeal were works for hire.

The judges confirmed that SRF could not renew copyrights that Yogananda had taken out in his books. But SRF could renew copyrights in articles that appeared in the SRF magazine, because SRF, as publisher, was the "proprietor" of the periodical. All articles that appeared in the magazine before 1943, however, were already in the public domain.

The opinion made short work of SRF's "works for hire" claim that Yogananda wrote as a mere employee of SRF, or under SRF's direction and control. The opinion noted that "Works motivated by Yogananda's own desire for self-expression or religious instruction of the public are not 'works for hire.' . . . Moreover, there was no evidence of supervision or control of Yogananda's work by SRF. Yogananda's works were thus not 'works for hire.'"

SRF's "corporate body" argument fared no better. The decision confirmed that this obscure doctrine applied only to a work when a group of affiliated individuals collaborated on a project without any one individual actually being the author of the work. The opinion agreed with Garcia that "SRF did not hold copyrights to Yogananda's works through the corporate body doctrine."

The Ninth Circuit's decision on whether Yogananda informally assigned his copyrights to SRF was less felicitous. We were told that SRF's copyrights could be valid if, before a work's first publication, Yogananda had in any way, *formally or otherwise*, assigned his common law rights to SRF. These common law assignments did not have to be in writing, and could be shown by oral statements, or even actions that merely implied an assignment, "without the necessity of observing any formalities." Schroeder concluded that, "The 1935 assignment is not dispositive as to Yogananda's writings after 1935, but it is relevant to this factual issue. While a jury may conclude that on balance the evidence demonstrates that Yogananda had no intent to transfer to SRF his common law copyrights, at the summary judgment stage, a district court is entitled neither to assess the weight of the conflicting evidence nor to make credibility determinations." So it came down to Yogananda's intentions, fifty years earlier, and a jury of strangers would have to decide what Yogananda meant based on snippets from his talks and newspaper clippings.

The articles in SRF's magazine were handled differently. The articles had been written by Yogananda, but were published in a "periodical" in which SRF, as its "proprietor," held the copyright. The 1909 Act allowed a proprietor to renew the copyright in its periodical as a whole. The proprietor's copyright had the effect of throwing a "blanket copyright" over the individual articles included in the magazine, so that they did not fall into the public domain after the initial registration term. The blanket copyright did not say who owned the copyrights in the articles—it simply preserved the owner's rights by preventing them from falling into the public domain. This resulted even when it was unclear who might own the actual copyright in any particular article. So the copyrights in Yogananda's contributions to the magazine had not fallen into the public domain. But who now owned them?

The opinion concluded:

> Thus, if SRF succeeds at trial in proving that Yogananda informally transferred to SRF his common law copyrights in his individual articles, SRF's blanket copyrights on each issue of its magazine were sufficient to give SRF rights to the articles as well. SRF would then have been entitled to renew these copyrights.

Yogananda had published three of his major works in serialized form: the "Second Coming of Christ," the "Spiritual Interpretation of the Bhagavad Gita," and "The Rubaiyat of Omar Khayyam." Most of these serialized works were now once again in play. The question of the ownership of the magazine articles were also being returned to Garcia so a jury could determine whether Yogananda had informally given these rights to SRF as well.

For the same reason the judges also reversed Garcia on the sound recordings. The 1909 Act did not cover new-fangled sound recordings, and SRF's rights in recordings of Yogananda's talks arose under California law. Garcia had correctly decided that Yogananda did not make the recorded talks as works for hire or as part of a corporate body. But because Yogananda might have informally assigned these rights to SRF as well, these too must be decided by the jury.

Finally, the opinion considered photographs of Yogananda that had appeared in SRF's magazine. SRF had no evidence on who took four of the photos, and the opinion affirmed Garcia's ruling on these four. *L.A. Times* staff photographer Arthur Say was not an SRF employee, and there was no evidence that he transferred his rights to SRF. The opinion accordingly affirmed Garcia's order that SRF held no rights in Arthur Say's "Last Smile" photographs. But Garcia's decision on four other photos, taken by SRF employees Clifford Frederick and Durga Mata, had to be reserved because his ruling was

> based on the court's rejection of the declaration of Ananda Mata, SRF's Secretary and Treasurer. The district court characterized Ananda Mata's declaration testimony as 'insufficient' and 'uncertain,' and commented on the possible inaccuracy of Ananda Mata's memory.

The Ninth Circuit reminded Garcia that for purposes of summary adjudication, he had to believe her declaration. And her declaration, true or not, was enough to send those four photos back to trial.

The decision in the second appeal was another victory, but a more limited one, and meant we must return to Sacramento for the trial we had hoped to avoid. It tantalized us with the prospect that the "jury may conclude that . . . Yogananda had no intent to transfer to SRF his common law copyrights." Now we would find out.

The Supreme Court Declines SRF's Invitation / Dec 2000

The appeal court's affirmation of Garcia's rulings must have appeared to SRF as writing on the wall. If the original works became public they would soon refute SRF's claim of "purity," and show instead its years of textual manipulation. SRF immediately asked the three-judge panel to rehear the case, and should they decline, SRF wanted a full review by the assembled circuit judges in the rarely used "en banc" process. An "en banc" rehearing occurs when an appellant asks all of the judges on the Ninth Circuit Court of Appeals to reconsider what a three-judge panel has decided. If a sufficient number of judges vote to hear the matter, a panel of eleven judges is chosen at random to hear arguments and reconsider the ruling. It seems the judges were satisfied with the decision as issued, however, and did not respond to SRF's request.

Undaunted, SRF petitioned the U.S. Supreme Court. The Supremes might yet set things right. But SRF faced a huge hurdle. Unlike that first appeal from the trial court, to which every party is entitled, you must petition the Supreme Court to grant you a "writ of certiorari" before they will take your case. That writ is the hallway pass that gets you to the courtroom where they will consider the merits of an appeal. Sometimes they grant a writ concerning only the issues that interest them, but usually they do nothing. Less than five percent of writ petitions are granted.

In its petition SRF raised the old arguments one last time. When the Supreme Court rejected the application—by a brusque postcard—this stage of the legal saga was finally over. The legal holdings of the second appeal became final for this case, and the law of the land. This 2000 decision, and its 1995 companion opinion, are cited often because they touched on many novel issues: use of generic and descriptive religious terms in trade names and trademarks, use of a religious leader's name as a service mark, copyrights under the 1909 Act in religious works made "for hire" and as a "corporate body," common law assignments under the 1909 Act, the legal effect of a swami's religious vows, and a religious corporation's claim to own the "name, voice, signature, photograph, or likeness" of its founder as a "deceased personality."

Chapter 15
THE FINAL FRAY
2001–2002

The decision in the second appeal freed many more writings and photographs, but sent part of the case back to Sacramento, so a jury could tell us whether Yogananda had informally assigned some writings to SRF. If the jury thought Yogananda meant the corporation to have his unpublished works and contributions to the magazine, SRF could reclaim something from its losses.

Ananda faced a difficult decision. Some suggested that we should stop actively defending the case entirely, and let SRF win what remained. Ananda had already won most of the issues: use of "Self-Realization"; use of Yogananda's name, voice, signature, photograph, and likeness; most of the photographs and numerous publications, including all of Yogananda's principal works. Along the way Ananda had obtained court orders invalidating SRF's service marks and trademarks.

Taking the case to trial would be costly. We could not do a jury trial in less than a month, living and working out of hotel rooms five days a week. Trial triggered a number of additional expenses, such as transporting witnesses, creating blow-ups and exhibits, and preparing witnesses to testify. Numerous motions and oppositions would be needed before trial, as well as legal briefs on specific issues of law that might arise along the way. And Ananda was already in debt.

Yet there were good reasons to press forward. Fruitless settlement talks had been conducted off and on ever since that first meeting in Fresno. After Ananda won the second summary adjudication motion, a representative from SRF had met with Ananda people in talks that first looked promising but went nowhere. The attempted settlement during the appeal also ended in disappointment. After Bertolucci, a negotiated settlement seemed unlikely. And to the extent that one of SRF's goals was to drive Ananda out of business through litigation costs, settlement would actually be counterproductive.

Moreover, the issues of the magazine still not in the public domain contained important texts, warranting additional effort to free them. Copyrights on portions of the "Second Coming" had already lapsed and those articles had been published by the Dallas-based Amrita Foundation. But most of the "Spiritual Interpretation of the Bhagavad Gita" and "The Rubaiyat of Omar Khayyam" would be available in their original form only if the magazine articles were freed from SRF's copyright claims.

In addition, there were doctrinal reasons for SRF to fight to keep the older periodicals out of general circulation. One of the principal differences between SRF and Ananda was Ananda's responsiveness to Yogananda's command to go forth in all directions and start "World Brotherhood Colonies." By the time of the lawsuit, SRF had long lost all interest in starting intentional communities.

Yogananda took advantage of the opportunity presented by a Sunday afternoon garden party in 1949, to issue one of his clearest calls for the formation of world brotherhood colonies. The party had been arranged by socialite and heiress Mrs. Clarence Myers to raise money for improvements to SRF's Sunset Boulevard church. The copper baron Isaac Guggenheim opened his thirty-two-room mansion for the affair, and decorated the house and grounds to resemble Tibetan gardens. Entertainment included the famous baritone Noel Cravat, as well as a dozen SRF monks who demonstrated yoga postures. The August 2, 1949 account in the Los Angeles Mirror, *related how the gala event was attended by "hundreds of socialites, film celebrities and just plain people." Near the end of his talk Yogananda announced that "This marks the birth of a new era." He explained:*

The word has been said, and we must go on—not only those who are here, but thousands of youths must go North, South, East and West to cover the earth with little colonies demonstrating that simplicity of living plus high thinking lead to the greatest happiness and strengthen character. Example talks louder than words. . . .

The Myers' party received a big write up in the November-December 1949 Self-Realization Magazine—*the event itself, quotations from Yogananda's talk, and three pages of photographs—detailing the significance of what was happening. After SRF decided far-flung villages did not fit within its corporate agenda, the party became simply another reminder of how things had changed.*

Yogananda's exhortation at the Myers' party would energize Ananda's founding of colonies around the world. But SRF still controlled the copyright to the article about the party. Kriyananda was present at the party and could talk all he wanted to about what he remembered Yogananda saying, but Ananda could not copy and distribute the magazine article or its copyrighted contents. Copying required SRF's permission, which would never be granted.

Ananda wanted to make these accounts of Yogananda's activities in the 1940s and early 1950s more public, to better explicate the final direction his mission had taken. Having come so far, after such an investment of time, money, and energy, it seemed worth the effort to try and free the full story.

There were other benefits. SRF would now, at long last, be required to show us the original manuscripts and typescripts of the "Second Coming" and the "Bhagavad Gita." These documents had been withheld from us during the prior years of litigation, but would have to be produced before trial. SRF claimed its possession of the original manuscripts evidenced the "informal assignment" of the common law copyright. After much negotiation and pointed correspondence, we arranged for a presentation and examination of the documents at the Richmond Temple, north of Berkeley. On May 13, 2002, just four months before the trial's start, the litigation team examined these original documents. It was a white glove affair. We could look at, but not touch, the manuscripts. Each page was turned at our request by an SRF monk in white gloves standing guard at the table. I could not help reflecting how the documents seemed more important to SRF than their content. SRF could coin new teachings as needed, but Yogananda's original writings were not so malleable. And here they were, presented in their pristine purity.

We broke into groups to review the materials. Still, it was slow going and took two full days. We had previously arranged who would be responsible for which documents, and agreed on what we were looking for. Having read so much about these works, their finalization out in the desert where Kriyananda and Tara Mata worked closely with Yogananda, and the still vague story of why they remained unpublished for fifty years, it was thrilling to finally see the originals. And SRF did indeed have possession of those original manuscripts. The fact that SRF held on to what Yogananda left behind, gave it a major leg up on its informal assignment claim. We never saw, however, the galley sheets that Yogananda told Rajarshi were ready for the press in 1951.

Durga and I worked together on chapters from the "Spiritual Interpretation of the Bhagavad Gita." The Gita is a very small slice from the immense *Mahabharata*, an epic of ancient India filled with amazing tales and allegorical stories. We are introduced to our heroes when the two armies have already assembled for battle on the plain of Kurukshetra, the Pandavas facing off against the Kauravas. The two sides comprised branches of royal cousins, caught up in a karmic soap opera of betrayal and skullduggery. Arjuna is a prince of the Pandavas, uncertain what to do now that taking action involves attacking his extended family. By luck he had drawn for his charioteer the God Krishna, the eighth avatar of Vishnu the preserver. In responding to Arjuna's questions, Krishna expounds a catechism of Yoga, Vedanta, and life: a précis of proper conduct in an uncertain world. The Gita speaks a lawyer's creed: duty in the face of adversity, effort without attachment to consequences. And propriety in all things, for as another part of the *Mahabharata* tells us, "Through dharmic action comes victory." Yogananda's exegesis applied the teachings of the Gita to the world around him, allowing the reader to draw new meaning from these ancient words. The Protective Order prevents me from saying more, but it was another amazing, once-in-a-lifetime opportunity.

Another perk of going forward was the chance to talk with some fascinating people we were thinking of calling as witnesses. Many were former disciples of Yogananda who never became SRF members, or who left after 1952. One larger-than-life figure was Herb Jeffries, "The Bronze Buckaroo." An early cowboy movie star of color, Jeffries headlined five Westerns in the late 1930s, billed as the "sensational singing cowboy." That voice opened other doors, and he left the movies to become a singer with the Duke Ellington Orchestra. He developed his own following over the years, and still actively performed, usually now for special events.

Jeffries had become a disciple of Yogananda in the late 1940s, after reading the *Autobiography* while convalescing in Michigan following an airplane crash. When he returned to the Los Angeles area, he sought out Yogananda and felt an instant bond. They would usually meet in the privacy of Yogananda's rooms on the third floor of Mt. Washington. Yogananda never encouraged Jeffries to join the organization, and preferred to maintain a personal direct relationship. Jeffries remained close to Yogananda through his final years, and was a favored guest at Yogananda's last birthday party on January 5, 1952. In a photo of the event that ran in the July-August 1952 issue of *Self-Realization Magazine,* he is shown sitting next to Yogananda. We thought Jeffries' experience illustrated how Yogananda maintained long-term personal interests outside the SRF organization. This in turn would permit the jury to infer that Yogananda maintained private financial and property interests outside the organization. In any event this charismatic character would be an entertaining witness. We prepared him to testify and gave him a subpoena, but he did not make the final cut of witnesses we called to the stand. His story of being a black actor in 1930s Los Angeles had gotten us thinking about what Yogananda must have experienced as a dark-skinned Indian, traveling around the country during the Roaring Twenties, the Depression, the New Deal, a world war, and then postwar America.

His celebrity status in later years might have protected him somewhat, but Yogananda was for many years an alien in America, and a Hindu to boot. At least until he became a US citizen later in life, Yogananda was subject to the California Alien Property Act, adopted by public acclaim in 1920. We stumbled across this fact in a letter written by Gyanamata to Nerode in 1935, one of many letters we obtained from third parties. She missed the Nerodes, and corresponded regularly with them as they moved from city to city spreading the Yogoda message in the 1920s and 1930s. Late in 1935, a week after Dhirananda entered judgment against Yogananda, Gyanamata wrote to Nerode in Ohio that the Mother Center was not concerned about Dhirananda attaching any property to satisfy the judgment. "The property belongs to the church, and Swamiji, being a Hindu, cannot, and never did, hold it."

We discovered that during these years the Alien Property Act prohibited the transfer of land to non-citizens, and aliens could not own real estate, unless they were eligible for citizenship. Asian nationalities were not eligible for citizenship, and thus could not own land. If an unauthorized alien attempted to take title to real property, it would become property of the state. The Alien Land Law remained in effect in California throughout Yogananda's lifetime. The California Supreme Court struck down part of the Act in 1952, before the voters repealed it entirely in 1956. So maybe there were other reasons Yogananda publicly stated he owned no property.

We were now fast approaching trial with a lot to do—preparing motions on evidence, jury instructions, examinations of witnesses, blow-up exhibits, and copies of the numerous documents to be shown witnesses. Rob and Richard had blended smoothly into the legal team over the years, and about this time we finalized that Rob would head up the team at trial. He would make the opening statement and the critical closing argument. He would also examine most of the witnesses, with Richard and me assisting as needed.

Fair Use / 2001–2002

SRF now turned the matter over to a group of strangers. Either side had the right to demand a jury, and SRF suspected what the result would be if Garcia decided the rest of the case. SRF had reserved the right to a jury when it first filed its complaint, and it now confirmed that the factual decisions would be out of Garcia's hands. Having laymen resolve this dispute also meant that the legal subtleties needed to be explained in ways the jury could grasp. We needed to explain the complicated history in terms of "themes" and "archetypes," craft examinations and arguments in ways that caught the jury's interest, and provide solutions that the jury could feel good adopting. We needed a simpler story, with a happy ending.

For the remaining writings at issue, Ananda had a first line argument and a fallback defense. First, we argued that SRF did not own any copyrights unless it had registered the work in its own name while Yogananda was still alive. We thought the facts showed that SRF was more the handy assistant than the bona fide inheritor of Yogananda's mission. He meant his works for the public, to be read as he wrote them. It was a good argument, but far from a sure winner, and we needed a fallback position.

SRF had facts that supported its claim to an implied assignment. It held the originals of the works, there were those numerous quotes of Yogananda saying he owned nothing because he had given everything to SRF, and written assignments of some specific personal property. We thought the finer grain of those facts showed that SRF had received only what Yogananda expressly gave it, that he spoke metaphorically about property ownership, and that he expressly kept the copyright to his principal writings in his own name. Ananda could not, of course, sift through SRF's archives and cull quotes that might set Yogananda's thinking in better focus, or clearly put the lie to SRF's half-truths. Still, we had done our homework and would put on a show.

We were confident concerning the photographs. They bore no hint who took them, or that they were taken at the direction of SRF. Other than Ananda Mata's impeached memory, SRF apparently had no evidence who took the photos, or under what circumstances. We expected, therefore, that SRF's claims to the photographs would fail at trial for lack of proof. Maybe the jury would see that SRF was overreaching, and therefore somehow less credible. But who knew what the jury would make of the history of these parties and their alien religion?

Our "Aw Shucks" defense to SRF's claim of intentional infringement, was the doctrine called "fair use." It provided that certain copying—for teaching, research, and the like—did not amount to illegal infringement. It used a "balancing test" that evaluated five elements to determine when copying crossed the line into infringement. We pushed hard on the doctrine in testimony from several sources, to give the jury leeway to let us off the hook, even if they thought SRF owned the copyrights. The 1909 Act did not define what it meant by "fair use," and over the years appellate decisions had given guidance on a case-by-case basis. We did not know how this jury would feel about fair use. It might come down to whether they saw Ananda's use of the works as a bona fide religious expression, or as the palming off that SRF alleged it to be.

Getting Ready / August 2002

The lawyers met with Judge Garcia on August 2, 2002, for the important pre-trial conference that had been put off years before. Garcia let us know that normally he holds these conferences in his chambers in a more relaxed setting, so the participants can get to know each other a bit better and smooth the mechanics of trial. For this case, however, the conference would be conducted in open court, every word taken down by a court reporter, "to be sure you behave." He set a brisk pace for required productions: all exhibits exchanged by September 10; motions on evidence filed by September 20 and any oppositions filed by September 25; proposed jury instructions lodged with the court and trial briefs filed and served by September 23. There were also witness lists, exhibit lists, and deposition excerpts that had to be prepared and exchanged before we could use them at trial.

The trial would begin Monday morning, September 30, 2002. We were to be there by 9:15, and Garcia would begin ruling on our motions at 9:30. We would then start picking a jury by 10:00. Garcia knew the two sides had each filed more than a dozen evidence motions, and he was giving us just two minutes per motion for our argument and his decision. We would go Monday through Friday beginning at 9:00 AM, except for Tuesdays and Thursdays, when we would start at 1:30. We agreed the trial would take about fifteen court days, to be spread over four weeks. Garcia wanted eight jurors rather than the usual minimum number of six, and he got them. In federal court a jury's decision must be unanimous, and because SRF bore the burden of proof, the greater the number of jurors, the harder its case became to win.

The evidence motions are called "motions in limine" and are decided just before trial begins. These motions ask the judge to rule beforehand that particular pieces of evidence will or will not be admissible, that specific questions may or may not be asked, or that certain events will not be discussed by counsel or witnesses within the jury's hearing. Such an order often involves instructing your client that they are not to spontaneously interject the prohibited information. The idea behind the motions is that you cannot "unring the bell" once irrelevant but prejudicial material has been paraded past the jury. Ananda raised 18 issues, and SRF 15, that we thought the judge should anticipate and address before testimony began. Having been burned by Bertolucci, some of our motions sought to prevent SRF from attacking Kriyananda again, or referring to Kriyananda's vows, Ananda's religious practices, or the Bertolucci case. We also used the motions in limine to try and exclude many of Yogananda's statements that he owned "nothing" or that he had given "everything" away.

SRF wanted to admit these quotes at trial because if Yogananda had given everything away, it supported SRF's argument that Yogananda gave everything to SRF. We pointed out that these statements were not literally true, Yogananda had *not*, in fact, given away all of his property. Ananda compiled substantial evidence that Yogananda continued to own and actively manage personal property and bank accounts throughout the time in question. Garcia knew of Yogananda's property ownership because Ananda had earlier used this evidence in support of a summary adjudication motion. Yogananda's statements about ownership on the material plane must be seen as metaphorical, as some form of affirmation, and an exhortation to non-attachment. Whatever he might have meant, it would be misleading for the jury to hear these quotes and take them for literal truth.

Moreover, their factual inaccuracy could be explained by their religious context. These statements were typically culled from some religious talk, or a letter written to encourage donations or respond to lawsuits. We argued that if the statements were made in a religious context, the court could not make secular sense out of them, at least not without impermissibly determining religious matters. Because we could not know what Yogananda meant by these statements, using them as evidence would mislead more than inform, and they should be excluded as unreliable and irrelevant. We filed our motions and made final preparations before decamping to the capitol.

Trial / Sept–Oct 2002

Everyone arrived in town the Friday before the Monday of trial to set up shop and make final arrangements. We were back at the Holiday Inn, just blocks from the new courthouse, with an additional suite for our "war room." Ananda stocked it with desks, computers, a printer, copier, and boxes upon boxes of materials gathered over the years. This was the nerve center where we discussed the next day's events, prepared witnesses, and wrote the last minute motions and papers that are required throughout a trial like this.

On September 30, 2002, trial finally began in the new courthouse. The building was a towering testament to justice in steel, wood, and glass, with an atrium evocative of a gothic cathedral. The nearby restaurants were not as good as those by the old courthouse, despite a mall across the street. But if I brought my suitcase to court on Friday, and no last minute matters arose, I could hop across the street and catch the 5:15 *Capitol Corridor* to the Bay Area, with a bar car to ease me through the delta and back home.

Flynn Thrown Out of Court / October 2002

During the morning break on one of the first days of testimony, I was walking down the window-walled corridor outside our eighth-floor courtroom when I heard Flynn's loud and unmistakable voice. It was booming through the open door of an attorney conference room. "Just say no! That's all you have to do, just say no!" As I walked past I turned my head and saw Flynn haranguing Brother Chidananda, the witness then still in the middle of testifying, who would retake the stand immediately after the break. It may surprise some, but there are limits to the ethical coaching of witnesses, called "woodshedding," and it sounded like Flynn had crossed that line. What surprised me, though, was that he did it shouting at a witness in a small room with an open door off the hallway next to the courtroom. What does that tell you? The door wide open. Compounding the folly was the fact that Garcia had already taken the trouble of prohibiting Flynn from officially appearing as SRF's counsel in the case. Flynn could not represent SRF in the courtroom, yet here he was, telling an SRF witness what to say when he resumed testifying.

As an officer of the court I had the pleasant duty of bringing such egregious misbehavior to Garcia's attention. His Honor was upset. We soon learned that Flynn had already caught Garcia's eye by what the judge described as flitting about the courtroom audience and "talking in stage whispers" so the jury could hear. Garcia called Flynn forward, and asked him to explain what he was doing. When Flynn started to explain, Garcia cut him off, and asked whether this was the same Michael Flynn the judge had earlier prohibited from appearing as *pro hac vice* counsel in the case. The exchange turned ugly, with Flynn sliding quickly from defensive, to combative, then loudly accusatory, and concluded with an angry Garcia ejecting Flynn from the courtroom. It was like a dramatic scripted scene out of a movie, only better because it was playing out live and unrehearsed before an enrapt audience. Garcia had pressed some hidden button and a burly Federal Marshal entered the courtroom, whereupon the judge instructed him, in a clear and forceful voice, that Flynn had been thrown out of this proceeding and was to leave the courtroom immediately. If Flynn did not leave, or if he tried to return to the courtroom, he was to be physically escorted from the building, with a marshal always in place to execute the order as needed. As Garcia talked the marshal adopted an aggressive arms-akimbo hand-near-the-gun posture, and began glaring at Flynn. Flynn would not back down, but ultimately stormed from the courtroom, ranting about "justice," with the marshal on his heels. As soon as the door closed behind them the entire audience broke into hushed conversations, requiring Garcia to gavel the proceedings back to order. It was better than the best Broadway.

But it wasn't all fun and games. The trial dragged on week after week. SRF effectively abandoned its claims to the remaining photographs and introduced no evidence showing that SRF, its employees, or its equipment had anything to do with any of the photos. Given the factual inconsistencies in Ananda Mata's earlier declarations and depositions, SRF decided not to call her as a witness, and Daya saw no reason to make the trip. Both begged off with letters from their doctors. SRF's evidence focused on the informal assignment, the audiotapes, and the magazine articles. We had not been able to exclude most of SRF's quotes and truncated comments about Yogananda giving everything away, and we were worried about their cumulative effect. We could not put the quotes in a more accurate context, or show why Yogananda had not meant that SRF should own all of his unpublished writings. The jury was getting tired. The lawyers were too. Late in the proceeding one of SRF's lawyers commented that he would pay to be able to get out of having to continue showing up day after day. I doubt any of us at Ananda's table felt that way. But I sympathized with the jury: the history was long and complex, the writings often obscure, and who really knew what Yogananda wanted when he left for the Biltmore on March 7, 1952? And SRF had possession of the original documents. SRF's story that Yogananda meant SRF to keep what he left behind provided an easy and satisfying way for the jury to wrap things up and return to their lives outside the courtroom.

In closing argument SRF asked the jury to award it over $33,000,000.00 as damages because Ananda had copied some of its magazine articles. Rather than try to prove that it had suffered any "actual damages," SRF elected to claim "statutory damages" in an amount fixed by law for each infringement. There were many little supposed infringements, and SRF wanted hundreds of dollars for each time anyone at Ananda copied anything from the magazines. After a decade of losses in court, SRF hoped for a knockout punch on damages for infringement of the magazine's articles. SRF could never collect tens of millions of dollars from Ananda, but the crushing debt might finally put Ananda out of business.

In the meantime more motions were called for. SRF had not introduced any evidence on the photographs, so Ananda brought a motion for "judgment as a matter of law" on those four remaining photographs, and Garcia granted that motion on October 24. Ananda had now won all of the photographs in the lawsuit. One of those photographs was labeled "PY, Myers Party." This was the photo of Yogananda's blessing given at the Myers' garden party in 1949, when Kriyananda heard his master call for people to go forth in all directions and start World Brotherhood Colonies.

Final Judgment / Oct–Dec 2002

The jury was out for days as we waited around, read the paper, strolled the hallway overlooking Sacramento, and made calls to kill time. On October 28, 2002, twelve years and three months after the complaint was filed, the jury returned a verdict. Their decision, with Solomon-like wisdom, gave SRF title to Yogananda's works on the basis of an implied common law assignment, including the articles in the magazines, but ruled that Ananda's use of those works had been a "fair use." There was no copyright infringement and, perhaps more importantly, no copyright damages.

The jury awarded SRF a total of $29,000 in damages for Ananda's use and sale of six audiotapes through time of trial. After twelve years of litigation SRF received damages insufficient to pay its legal fees for a week of trial. The clerk entered judgment on this part of the case the next day. SRF won only the common law copyrights in the magazine and audiotapes. The jury did not validate SRF as Yogananda's successor, but rather determined that among the things Yogananda left behind on March 7, 1952, were his common law copyrights. SRF managed to keep the copyrights in the magazine articles and audio recordings for their statutory renewal periods, and the rights in any unpublished writings and talks for so long as they remain unpublished. These rights, though overshadowed by SRF's losses, were significant because they allowed SRF to control the editing and future release of materials not yet in the public domain.

The judge's gavel after the jury verdict did not, however, end the proceedings. Additional issues still had to be worked out by counsel, or decided by the judge. The final judgment's language needed drafting, and post-trial motions might be required, including both sides' requests for legal fees. SRF was already talking about another appeal.

Ananda stood ready to take the high road home from court. We were happy with the result and weary of the fight. The parties met in strained but productive sessions and in less than two months worked out the terms of a judgment that cobbled together various prior rulings and opinions, and that waived all appeals and post-trial motions. SRF had asked Garcia for "declaratory relief" in the form of a statement that SRF was the owner of certain rights in the magazine articles and the audiotapes. When Garcia signed and entered the four page "Final Judgment Terminating Action" in December 2002, he ruled that SRF owned the copyrights in the following works: (a) nine article series and works appearing in SRF's magazine between 1943 and 1976, and (b) six sound recordings of Yogananda made between 1949 and 1951. One of the articles successfully retained by SRF was the account in *Self-Realization Magazine* of Yogananda's talk given at Myers' garden party. SRF could still keep some things out of the light, and its many hidden treasures remained secure. After twelve years of litigation SRF had managed not to lose everything. Mission accomplished.

The Final Judgment also confirmed the earlier surviving orders and rulings in Ananda's favor. Taking all the rulings and results into account, Ananda appeared to have won much and lost little, coming out well on top. Garcia seemed to agree because after the verdict he once stated he "assumed" Ananda would be bringing a motion for its fees. Attorneys' fees by this time were a very big deal. The "prevailing party" was entitled to its legal fees on many of SRF's claims together with certain out-of-pocket expenses. Even if some of the legal fees might not be recoverable, with the final number dependent on the judge's discretion, Ananda still stood to recover many of the millions paid over the years. These fees would dwarf the $29,000 in damages.

But requesting fees and costs meant more motions, and SRF would surely appeal any award. After much discussion and reflection, Ananda agreed to give up its claim to fees and costs if it would buy peace. It did. Both sides waived all post-trial motions and rights of appeal, gave up all claims to fees and costs, and agreed that entry of judgment would "represent the final termination of this action." On December 16, 2002, Garcia approved the final form of the judgment, signed it, and had it entered by the clerk. The case was over. It was my birthday.

Some months afterwards I read a "Judicial Profile" in the daily legal newspaper about Judge Garcia. It quoted him as saying that he did not like jury trials for copyright cases, because the jury always seemed to get it wrong. I think he had our case in mind. When asked for the names of some representative cases he had presided over, he included the SRF lawsuit with Ananda high on his short list.

Karma Kicks Back / Dec 2002 and beyond

The lawsuit hurt SRF with bad press and defections from its ranks. I never thought karma could kick back so quickly. Reporters started snooping around SRF and uncovering more inconvenient facts. In July 1999, for example, Ron Russell broke the story in the *Los Angeles New Times* that Daya Mata and Ananda Mata were no longer living on Mt.

Washington. Tobacco heiress Doris Duke had made it possible for the sisters to move to a nice house on the 200 block of South Canon Avenue in Sierra Madre—with enough money to buy a place next door to house the monastic help.

SRF's litigious energy attracted new lawsuits. In 1994 SRF was sued in Kern County, California and in New York by decedents' estates over bequests made to the organization, and a similar federal lawsuit followed in 2000. In 1998 an SRF member named Patricia Lyons sued the organization for sexual harassment, and garnered a settlement rumored to be $333,000. The next year Sunset Palisades filed suit, followed by several injury and employment claims, as SRF continued to reap what it had sowed. These years took a terrible internal toll on SRF as well. Between 2000 and 2005 more than fifty monks and nuns are reported to have left the organization.

During the lawsuit, with Ananda's assistance, Joan Wight published a three-part memoir written by Durga Mata, a nun who joined Yogananda in December 1929. SRF tried to stop the publication of this *Trilogy of Divine Love*, and claimed that Durga Mata's writings also belonged to the corporation. But Joan produced a 1975 Confirmation of Gift in which Durga Mata specifically included her writings as part of her gift to Joan. Following a pointed letter from Joan's lawyers, SRF backed down.

The struggle may have stirred SRF to some action. In response to Ananda's release of audio recordings, SRF also published those same recordings, and a few more as well. Even so, the recordings released by SRF are nothing compared with the wealth of material still withheld. One might expect SRF eager to share its Master's vocal vibrations with the world, to get the real deal out there in the cosmos. Yet SRF has released only ten CDs of Yogananda's talks, this small number reflecting, perhaps, that it is harder to edit audio recordings than writings. SRF also spiffed up the magazine and, after half a century of delay, published a version of Yogananda's commentary on the Bhagavad Gita, entitled *God Talks With Arjuna*. As SRF learned that Ananda was about to release a work, like the *Rubaiyat*, it would rush its own version to press and grab shelf space in the bookstores. Thus, the lawsuit urged SRF's discipleship on to greater, if spiteful, zeal, and resulted in the completion of works that had languished for years. Perhaps the real beneficiary of the lawsuits is the public at large, who now has access to these materials concerning Yogananda and his teachings.

The Last Smile / 2002

Ananda's efforts resulted in many photos being recognized as public domain images. My favorite was the famous final photo of Yogananda called "The Last Smile." *L.A. Times* photographer Arthur Say snapped it while on assignment at the Biltmore on March 7, 1952. He was there to take photos for the paper's planned story about the dinner honoring Indian Ambassador Binay Ranjan Sen, at which Yogananda would speak. Just before being called to the dais to be seated next to the ambassador's wife, Yogananda let Say take a series of four photos. These photos of a benign, smiling Yogananda capture the guru's final expression just moments before his *mahasamadhi*. SRF had claimed for years that it owned the copyright to the photo, sued Ananda for their use of it, and had threatened others into inaction. We now know that SRF does not have the copyright. When Ananda concluded the lawsuit, I like to think they walked away with the Last Smile.

AFTERWORD

2002 and beyond

It was litigation larger than life, in which we wrestled with the angels of religious freedom and with *karma*, while greater events spun about us. We were sometimes confused, if not disheartened, but pushed as duty called, always toward the light as best we could see it. The litigation spanned more than a decade and proved a transforming experience for everyone involved. Ananda tore away the veil of secrecy around SRF, and made Yogananda's teachings available for the world. In its attempt to present a single manicured image of Yogananda, SRF triggered an explosion of books, articles, and blogs that revealed the original teachings and started open discussions about Yogananda and his organizations.

Every story is a personal one, with victories and defeats, and going on regardless. I thought all along that the litigation was about the freedom of religion under the law, and the freedom of churches, teachers, and followers to express their truth as they understood it. It was about the personal trials and spiritual growth of a devoted disciple doing his Master's work, who might be more like his Master than he imagined. It was about the bright-eyed, earnest souls at Ananda whose many hands made miracles. It was certainly about all that. And much more, beyond my ability to take the measure of such things, or know what they might mean.

I had hoped that we were holding up a mirror to SRF, giving the Matas a chance to see what they were doing, and an opportunity to change. But it was too late for that. Daya Mata was a loyal devoted administrator who had been given more than she could manage. Concerned about the spelling of Paramhansa she abruptly changed it, which meant that Yogananda's signature had to be altered as well. She fretted about photos showing Yogananda wearing a cross, and airbrushed out the Christianity. She doubted herself, and manipulated Yogananda's writings to buttress the power of her position. Unsure of the teachings' direction, she withheld works that Yogananda had readied for the press before his passing. To preclude other teachers outshining her, she changed who could teach Kriya, give lessons, and publish writings. Fearing some other organization might supplant SRF, she threatened or sued them, asserting questionable claims through troublesome actions. I guess it worked for her. Now that she has passed we will see what direction SRF takes.

I thought we were making a difference. And maybe we did. For Ananda no longer stands in the shadow of SRF. SRF's attempt to control everything about Yogananda, his teachings, his writings, and his mission, was rebuffed and religious freedom won a round. But all I really know is that for a while we struggled together as brothers and sisters in arms, did our best, and did some good. That's enough for me.

Everyone who played a part in the litigation helped shape Ananda into what it is today. Those twelve years of lawsuits and appeals were traumatic at the time, but have borne fruit in an expanded and invigorated community. As special as those years were, the litigation was just another of the many challenges and crises that have shaped the direction of Ananda's mission. As treasured as those memories are, Ananda's most exciting days are still to come.

On January 3, 2003, Ananda sent out the last case update to Ananda's supporters announcing the end of the lawsuit. There were still bills to pay but the bleeding had stopped, and it was time to mend. Its concluding comments expressed a sentiment I heard from many at Ananda during the lawsuit, and from everyone since the judgment:

> Now that the long, costly lawsuit has finally ended, we at Ananda hope that there can be increasing harmony between the two organizations in the years to some, and that we can, in time, become friends. We . . . extend our sincere love and friendship to all our gurubais (fellow disciples) in Self-Realization Fellowship, and everywhere.

WHERE ARE THEY NOW?

Swami Kriyananda

Between the end of the SRF lawsuit and now, Swami Kriyananda has continued to serve his guru, Paramhansa Yogananda, by helping many thousands of people progress on the path of Self-realization. In addition to traveling around the globe every year and giving frequent talks on his guru's teachings in America, Europe, and India, in recent years Kriyananda (a prolific author of more than 140 titles) has written over 30 new books, including *The New Path: My Life with Paramhansa Yogananda* (which has received two book awards) and *Paramhansa Yogananda: A Biography with Personal Reflections and Reminiscences* (which received the 2012 International Book Award for Best New Spirituality Book). Swamiji has also founded a new religious (Nayaswami) order that encourages both single and married people to live their lives for God, and has written three scripts for upcoming feature films on the life and teachings of Paramhansa Yogananda. In 2012, Swami Kriyananda turned 86.

Sheila Rush

Following the SRF court case, Sheila "Naidhruva" Rush has served as editor of Ananda's quarterly publication, *Clarity Magazine*, which in 2009 became an online only magazine. Since 2009, *Clarity's* readership has increased from 1500 to nearly 9000 worldwide, and continues to grow. *Clarity* features articles by Paramhansa Yogananda, Swami Kriyananda, and other Ananda teachers, which discuss spiritual principles and the application of spiritual principles to everyday life.

Cathy Parojinog

In May 2004, Cathy "Latika" Parojinog was appointed treasurer, and became the chief financial officer of Ananda Church of Self-Realization of Nevada County. She also served as corporate secretary until June 2006, when she became general manager of Ananda, was elected to the board of directors, and appointed vice-president.

Keshava

Along with his wife Daya, Keshava Taylor is currently fulfilling ministerial duties in India, serving Ananda's work there, giving talks on Yogananda's teachings and leading pilgrimages to Yogananda's sacred sites.

Ananda

Ananda has blossomed since the end of the SRF court case. New Ananda communities have begun in Los Angeles, California, and in Gurgaon and Pune, India. New Ananda centers and meditation groups have been founded all over the world. Ananda ministers regularly travel to visit these groups and centers, giving talks and Sunday services. Many thousands are helped by these activities, and even more through Ananda's website, www.ananda.org, where 400,000 people visit yearly to enjoy the free videos and web pages sharing Yogananda's teachings.

Daya Mata

After 55 years as president of Self-Realization Fellowship, Daya Mata passed away on November 30, 2010.

Ananda Mata

Sister of Daya Mata, and longtime treasurer and member of the SRF Board of Directors, Ananda Mata left her body on February 5, 2005.

Mrinalini Mata

After the passing of Daya Mata in 2010, Mrinalini Mata assumed the duties of president of Self-Realization Fellowship.

SRF

Following the end of its lawsuit against Ananda, Self-Realization Fellowship has continued its work through its publications, and its centers and meditation groups worldwide—and has not taken any other spiritual organizations to court.

Relations between Ananda and SRF

Since the end of the lawsuit in 2002, there has been no substantive improvement in communication between the two organizations. Ananda continues to reach out to improve cooperation and harmony.

Robert A. Christopher

Rob is now Of Counsel with the San Jose law firm of Hopkins and Carley, and has started his own dispute resolution organization, "Just Resolve," a lawyer-free dispute resolution service. He divides the rest of his time between the Christopher Ranch family business and the South Valley Civic Theater.

Richard A. Jones

Richard is currently Special Counsel and Litigation Manager in the San Francisco office of the international law firm of Covington & Burling, LLP. He advises on employment, intellectual property, commercial, antitrust, and business matters in federal and state courts, at both the trial court and appellate levels.

Gordon L. Rockhill

Gordon retired from the practice of law a few years after the Bertolucci lawsuit and now indulges his passion for woodworking.

Judge Edward J. Garcia

Judge Garcia assumed senior status on November 24, 1996, but still handles cases daily in the U.S. District Court in Sacramento.

Judge Lawrence T. Stevens

Judge Stevens was appointed to the First District Court of Appeal on August 15, 1998. He retired in 2007, and is no longer an active member of the bar.

ABOUT THE AUTHOR

Jon R. Parsons, founder of the Jon R. Parsons Law Firm in Palo Alto, California, has provided legal services in the San Francisco Bay Area for over thirty years. Mr. Parsons has extensive experience advising both charitable and for-profit organizations, and has represented many religious entities in the U.S. and overseas. With an academic background in Chinese and Indian Studies, Mr. Parsons received his Bachelor of Arts degree from the University of Illinois, and attended the University of Chicago for his graduate studies. He received his Juris Doctor from the Santa Clara University School of Law.

Mr. Parsons, a Mensa member, spearheaded Ananda's defense in court against Self-Realization Fellowship. This is his first book.

INDEX

Thanks to the lawsuit

CRYSTAL CLARITY

is honored to be able to present
the following titles

The original 1946 unedited edition of Yogananda's spiritual masterpiece

AUTOBIOGRAPHY OF A YOGI
by Paramhansa Yogananda

Autobiography of a Yogi is one of the best-selling Eastern philosophy titles of all time, with millions of copies sold, named one of the best and most influential books of the twentieth century. This highly prized reprinting of the original 1946 edition is the only one available free from textual changes made after Yogananda's death. Yogananda was the first yoga master of India whose mission was to live and teach in the West.

In this updated edition are bonus materials, including a last chapter that Yogananda wrote in 1951, without posthumous changes. This new edition also includes the eulogy that Yogananda wrote for Gandhi, and a new foreword and afterword by Swami Kriyananda, one of Yogananda's close, direct disciples. Also available in unabridged audiobook (MP3) format, read by Swami Kriyananda, Yogananda's direct disciple.

"In the original edition, published during Yogananda's life, one is more in contact with Yogananda himself."
—David Frawley, Director, American Institute of Vedic Studies, author of *Yoga and Ayurveda*

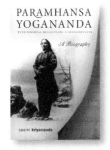

PARAMHANSA YOGANANDA
A Biography with Personal Reflections and Reminiscences
by Swami Kriyananda

Paramhansa Yogananda's classic *Autobiography of a Yogi* is more about the saints Yogananda met than about himself—in spite of the fact that Yogananda was much greater than many he described. Now, one of Yogananda's few remaining direct disciples relates the untold story of this great spiritual master and world teacher: his teenage miracles, his challenges in coming to America, his national lecture campaigns, his struggles to fulfill his world-changing mission amid incomprehension and painful betrayals, and his ultimate triumphant achievement. Kriyananda's subtle grasp of his guru's inner nature reveals Yogananda's many-sided greatness. Includes many never-before-published anecdotes.

THE NEW PATH

My Life with Paramhansa Yogananda
by Swami Kriyananda

This is the moving story of Kriyananda's years with Paramhansa Yogananda, India's emissary to the West and the first yoga master to spend the greater part of his life in America. When Swami Kriyananda discovered *Autobiography of a Yogi* in 1948, he was totally new to Eastern teachings. This is a great advantage to the Western reader, since Kriyananda walks us along the yogic path as he discovers it from the moment of his initiation as a disciple of Yogananda. With winning honesty, humor, and deep insight, he shares his journey on the spiritual path through personal stories and experiences. Through more than four hundred stories of life with Yogananda, we tune in more deeply to this great master and to the teachings he brought to the West. This book is an ideal complement to *Autobiography of a Yogi*.

2013 PARAMHANSA YOGANANDA CALENDAR

Enjoy the blessings of the great world teacher Paramhansa Yogananda all year round through this gorgeous wall calendar. Each month features a special sepia-toned photograph of the yoga master and features an inspiring and enlightening quote from his writings. The calendar makes a perfect gift for all your spiritual friends and family, a wonderful way to be uplifted each and every day of the year.

THE ESSENCE OF THE BHAGAVAD GITA

Explained by Paramhansa Yogananda
As Remembered by his disciple, Swami Kriyananda

Rarely in a lifetime does a new spiritual classic appear that has the power to change people's lives and transform future generations. This is such a book. This revelation of India's best-loved scripture approaches it from a fresh perspective, showing its deep allegorical meaning and its down-to-earth practicality. The themes presented are universal: how to achieve victory in life in union with the divine; how to prepare for life's "final exam," death, and what happens afterward; how to triumph over pain and suffering.

"A brilliant text that will greatly enhance the spiritual life of every reader."
—Caroline Myss, author of *Anatomy of the Spirit* and *Sacred Contracts*

"It is doubtful that there has been a more important spiritual writing in the last fifty years than this soul-stirring, monumental work. What a gift! What a treasure!"
—Neale Donald Walsch, author of *Conversations with God*

THE BHAGAVAD GITA
According to Paramhansa Yogananda
Edited by Swami Kriyananda

This translation of the Gita, by Paramhansa Yogananda, brings alive the deep spiritual insights and poetic beauty of the famous battlefield dialogue between Krishna and Arjuna. Based on the little-known truth that each character in the Gita represents an aspect of our own being, it expresses with revelatory clarity how to win the struggle within between the forces of our lower and higher natures.

REVELATIONS OF CHRIST
Proclaimed by Paramhansa Yogananda
Presented by his disciple, Swami Kriyananda

The rising tide of alternative beliefs proves that now, more than ever, people are yearning for a clear-minded and uplifting understanding of the life and teachings of Jesus Christ. This galvanizing book, presenting the teachings of Christ from the experience and perspective of Paramhansa Yogananda, one of the greatest spiritual masters of the twentieth century, finally offers the fresh perspective on Christ's teachings for which the world has been waiting. *Revelations of Christ* presents us with an opportunity to understand and apply the scriptures in a more reliable way than any other: by studying under those saints who have communed directly, in deep ecstasy, with Christ and God.

"This is a great gift to humanity. It is a spiritual treasure to cherish and to pass on to children for generations." —Neale Donald Walsch, author of *Conversations with God*

"Kriyananda's revelatory book gives us the enlightened, timeless wisdom of Jesus the Christ in a way that addresses the challenges of twenty-first century living." —Michael Beckwith, Founder and Spiritual Director, Agape International Spiritual Center, author of *Inspirations of the Heart*

THE RUBAIYAT OF OMAR KHAYYAM EXPLAINED
Paramhansa Yogananda, edited by Swami Kriyananda

The Rubaiyat is loved by Westerners as a hymn of praise to sensual delights. In the East its quatrains are considered a deep allegory of the soul's romance with God, based solely on the author Omar Khayyam's reputation as a sage and mystic. But for centuries the meaning of this famous poem has remained a mystery. Now Yogananda reveals the secret meaning and the golden spiritual treasures hidden behind the Rubaiyat's verses, and presents a new scripture to the world.

GOD IS FOR EVERYONE
Inspired by Paramhansa Yogananda
by Swami Kriyananda

This book presents a concept of God and spiritual meaning that will broadly appeal to everyone, from the most uncertain agnostic to the most fervent believer. Clearly and simply written, thoroughly non-sectarian and non-dogmatic in its approach, it is the perfect introduction to the spiritual path.

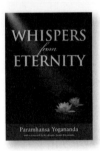

WHISPERS FROM ETERNITY
Paramhansa Yogananda, edited by his disciple, Swami Kriyananda

Many poetic works can inspire, but few, like this one, have the power to change your life. Yogananda was not only a spiritual master, but a master poet, whose verses revealed the hidden divine presence behind even everyday things. This book has the power to rapidly accelerate your spiritual growth, and provides hundreds of delightful ways for you to begin your own conversation with God.

THE ESSENCE OF SELF-REALIZATION
The Wisdom of Paramhansa Yogananda

*Recorded, Compiled, and Edited
by his disciple Swami Kriyananda*

With nearly three hundred of Paramhansa Yogananda's sayings rich with spiritual wisdom, this book is the fruit of a labor of love by his disciple, Swami Kriyananda. A glance at the table of contents will convince the reader of the vast scope of this book. It offers as complete an explanation of life's true purpose, and of the way to achieve that purpose, as may be found anywhere.

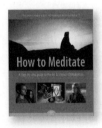

HOW TO MEDITATE
A Step-by-Step Guide to the Art & Science of Meditation
by Jyotish Novak

This clear and concise guidebook has helped thousands since it was first published in 1989. With easy-to-follow instructions, meditation teacher Jyotish Novak demystifies meditation—presenting the essential techniques so that you can quickly grasp them. This newly revised edition includes a bonus chapter on scientific studies showing the benefits of meditation, plus all-new photographs and illustrations.

Swami Kriyananda (J. Donald Walters)

CONVERSATIONS WITH YOGANANDA

Recorded, Compiled, and Edited
with commentary by his disciple, Swami Kriyananda

This is an unparalleled, first-hand account of the teachings of Paramhansa Yogananda. Featuring nearly 500 never-before-released stories, sayings, and insights, this is an extensive, yet eminently accessible treasure trove of wisdom from one of the 20th Century's most famous yoga masters.

Through these *Conversations*, Yogananda comes alive. Time and space dissolve. We sit at the feet of the Master, listen to his words, receive his wisdom, delight in his humor, and are transformed by his love.

"A wonderful book! To find a previously unknown message from Yogananda now is an extraordinary spiritual gift. Open up at random for an encouraging word from one of the century's most beloved spiritual teachers." —Neale Donald Walsch, author of *Conversations with God*

~ THE WISDOM OF YOGANANDA SERIES ~

Six volumes of Paramhansa Yogananda's timeless wisdom in an approachable, easy-to-read format. The writings of the Master are presented with minimal editing, to capture his expansive and compassionate wisdom, his sense of fun, and his practical spiritual guidance.

HOW TO BE HAPPY ALL THE TIME

The Wisdom of Yogananda Series, VOLUME 1

Yogananda powerfully explains virtually everything needed to lead a happier, more fulfilling life. Topics include: looking for happiness in the right places; choosing to be happy; tools and techniques for achieving happiness; sharing happiness with others; balancing success and happiness; and many more.

KARMA & REINCARNATION

The Wisdom of Yogananda Series, VOLUME 2

Yogananda reveals the truth behind karma, death, reincarnation, and the afterlife. With clarity and simplicity, he makes the mysterious understandable. Topics include: why we see a world of suffering and inequality; how to handle the challenges in our lives; what happens at death; and the purpose of reincarnation.

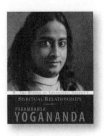

SPIRITUAL RELATIONSHIPS
The Wisdom of Yogananda Series, VOLUME 3

This book contains practical guidance and fresh insight on relationships of all types. Topics include: how to cure bad habits that can end true friendship; how to choose the right partner; sex in marriage and how to conceive a spiritual child; problems that arise in marriage; the Universal Love behind all your relationships.

HOW TO BE A SUCCESS
The Wisdom of Yogananda Series, VOLUME 4

This book includes the complete text of *The Attributes of Success*, the original booklet later published as *The Law of Success*. In addition, you will learn how to find your purpose in life, develop habits of success and eradicate habits of failure, develop your will power and magnetism, and thrive in the right job.

HOW TO HAVE COURAGE, CALMNESS, & CONFIDENCE
The Wisdom of Yogananda Series, VOLUME 5

Winner of the 2011 International Book Award
~ Best Self-Help Title ~

This book shows you how to transform your life. Dislodge negative thoughts and depression. Uproot fear and thoughts of failure. Cure nervousness and systematically eliminate worry from your life. Overcome anger, sorrow, over-sensitivity, and a host of other troublesome emotional responses; and much more.

HOW TO ACHIEVE GLOWING HEALTH & VITALITY
The Wisdom of Yogananda Series, VOLUME 6

Paramhansa Yogananda, a foremost spiritual teacher of modern times, offers practical, wide-ranging, and fascinating suggestions on how to have more energy and live a radiantly healthy life. The principles in this book promote physical health and all-round well-being, mental clarity, and ease and inspiration in your spiritual life. Readers will discover the priceless Energization Exercises for rejuvenating the body and mind, the fine art of conscious relaxation, and helpful diet tips for health and beauty.

PLEASE VISIT OUR WEBSITE to view our many other titles in books, music, audiobooks, e-books, spoken word, and DVDs: **www.crystalclarity.com**

CRYSTAL CLARITY PUBLISHERS

Crystal Clarity Publishers offers additional resources to assist you in your spiritual journey including many other books, a wide variety of inspirational and relaxation music composed by Swami Kriyananda, and yoga and meditation videos. To see a complete listing of our products, contact us for a print catalog or see our website: www.crystalclarity.com

Crystal Clarity Publishers
14618 Tyler Foote Rd., Nevada City, CA 95959
TOLL FREE: 800.424.1055 or 530.478.7600 / FAX: 530.478.7610
EMAIL: clarity@crystalclarity.com

ANANDA WORLDWIDE

Ananda Sangha, a worldwide organization founded by Swami Kriyananda, offers spiritual support and resources based on the teachings of Paramhansa Yogananda. There are Ananda spiritual communities in Nevada City, Sacramento, and Palo Alto, California; Seattle, Washington; Portland, Oregon; as well as a retreat center and European community in Assisi, Italy, and communities near New Delhi and Pune, India. Ananda supports more than 75 meditation groups worldwide.

For more information about Ananda Sangha communities or meditation groups near you, please call 530.478.7560 or visit www.ananda.org

THE EXPANDING LIGHT

Ananda's guest retreat, The Expanding Light, offers a varied, year-round schedule of classes and workshops on yoga, meditation, and spiritual practice. You may also come for a relaxed personal renewal, participating in ongoing activities as much or as little as you wish. The beautiful serene mountain setting, supportive staff, and delicious vegetarian food provide an ideal environment for a truly meaningful, spiritual vacation.

For more information, please call 800.346.5350 or visit www.expandinglight.org